my **revision** notes

WJEC GCSE HISTORY

R. Paul Evans

HODDER EDUCATION
AN HACHETTE UK COMPANY

For my parents, Ron and Beryl Evans, in appreciation of their continuous support and encouragement during my university education and subsequent historical research.

The publishers would like to thank the following for permission to reproduce copyright material:

Photo credits

p.14 © 1999 Credit: Topham Picturepoint/TopFoto; **p.49** © Corbis; **p.72** 'They salute with both hands now' by David Low published in London Evening Standard 3 July 1934 © Solo Syndication / Associated Newspapers Ltd. (photo: British Cartoon Archive, University of Kent); **p. 107** © George Marks/Retrofile/Getty Images

Every effort has been made to trace all copyright holders, but if any have been inadvertently overlooked the Publishers will be pleased to make the necessary arrangements at the first opportunity.

Although every effort has been made to ensure that website addresses are correct at time of going to press, Hodder Education cannot be held responsible for the content of any website mentioned in this book. It is sometimes possible to find a relocated web page by typing in the address of the home page for a website in the URL window of your browser.

Hachette UK's policy is to use papers that are natural, renewable and recyclable products and made from wood grown in sustainable forests. The logging and manufacturing processes are expected to conform to the environmental regulations of the country of origin.

Orders: please contact Bookpoint Ltd, 130 Milton Park, Abingdon, Oxon OX14 4SB. Telephone: +44 (0)1235 827720. Fax: +44 (0)1235 400454. Lines are open 9.00a.m.–5.00p.m., Monday to Saturday, with a 24-hour message answering service. Visit our website at www.hoddereducation.co.uk.

First published in 2012 by
Hodder Education,
an Hachette UK company
338 Euston Road
London NW1 3BH

Impression number 10 9 8 7 6 5

Year 2017 2016 2015 2014 2013

Cover photo : © Lantapix/Alamy

Typeset in 11/13 Frutiger LT Std by Datapage (India) Pvt. Ltd.
Artwork by Datapage, Barking Dog and Gray Publishing.
Printed and bound in Spain

A catalogue record for this title is available from the British Library.

ISBN 978 1 444 15857 1

Get the most from this book

This book will help you revise for the WJEC GCSE History specification, which can be downloaded from the WJEC website www.wjec.co.uk. Follow the links to GCSE History Specification.

This book covers the Depth Studies of **Russia in transition, 1914–1924, The USA: a nation of contrasts, 1910–1929** and **Germany in transition, c.1929–1947** and the Development Study **The development of the USA, 1929–2000**.

You can use the revision planner on pages 4 and 5 to plan your revision, topic by topic. Tick each box when you have:

1. revised and understood a topic
2. answered the exam practice questions
3. checked your answers online.

You can also keep track of your revision by ticking off each topic heading throughout the book. Be a scribbler, make notes as you learn. You will need an exercise book for most of the revision tasks, but you can also write in this book.

Tick to track your progress

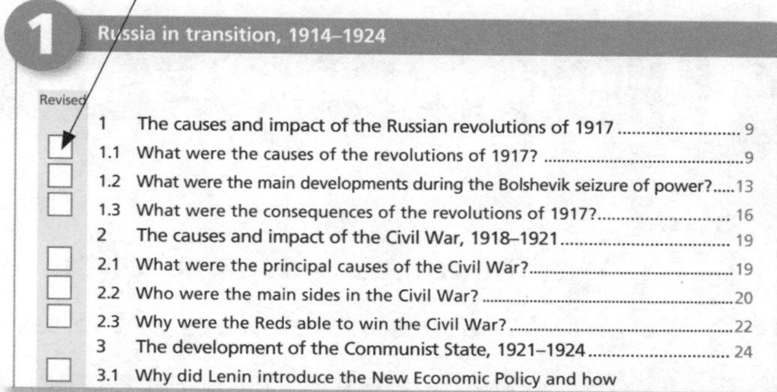

1 Russia in transition, 1914–1924

Revised

Revision tasks

Use these tasks to make sure that you have understood every topic and to help you think about what you are revising. If you do the tasks you will have to use the information in the book. If you use the information you will remember it better. The more you use the information the better you will remember it.

Tick to track your progress

Key issues

Key issues from the specification are listed on the first page of each chapter. You need to have a good knowledge and understanding of these key issues.

Key terms

Key terms are **highlighted** the first time they appear, with an explanation nearby in the margin.

Exam practice

Sample exam questions are provided for each topic. Use them to consolidate your revision and practise your exam skills.

Go online

Go online to check your answers to the exam questions and try out the quick quizzes at **www.therevisionbutton.co.uk/myrevisionnotes**.

Examiner's tip

Throughout the book there are examiner's tips that explain how you can boost your final grade.

Contents and revision planner

3 Germany in transition, *c.*1929–1947

4 The development of the USA, 1929–2000

Introduction

How to revise

There is no single way to revise, but here are some good ideas.

1. Make a revision timetable

For a subject like history, which involves learning large amounts of factual detail, it is essential that you construct a 'revision plan':

- **Start early** – you should start by looking at the dates of your exams and work backwards to the first date you intend to start revising, probably 6 to 8 weeks before your exam.
- **Be realistic** – work out a realistic revision plan to complete your revision; don't try to do too much. Remember that you have to fit in your history revision alongside your other GCSE subjects. Plan to include breaks to give yourself a rest.
- **Revise regularly** – regular, short spells of 40 minutes are better than panicky six-hour slogs until 2a.m.
- **Plan your time carefully** – give more revision time to topic areas you find difficult and spend longer on the sections you feel less confident about.
- **Track your progress** – keep to your timetable, and use the revision planner on pages 4 and 5 to tick off each topic as you complete it. Give yourself targets and reward yourself when you have achieved them.

2. Revise actively

Different people revise in different ways and you will have to find the methods which best suit your learning style. Here are some techniques which students have used to help them revise:

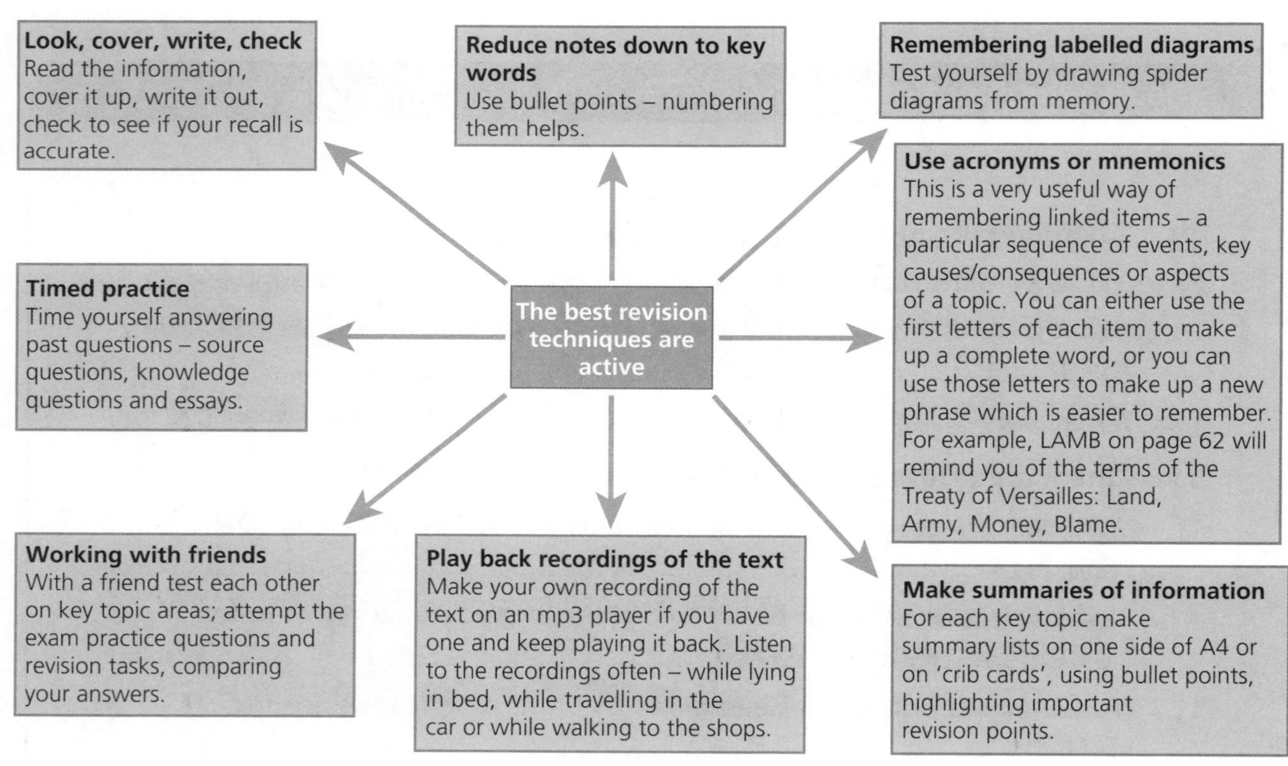

How to prepare for the exam

1. Decode the exam question – look for the 'command' words

To perform well in the exam, you will have to answer the questions correctly. The key to success is understanding what the question is asking – look for the key command words which will tell you the type of answer you should write.

Common command words and what they mean:

Explain	Provide a number of reasons, showing how or why each contributed to the event named in the question.
Describe	Provide specific factual detail upon the key issue named in the question.
How important ... **How successful ...** **How far ...**	Provide a judgement upon the named event/person supported by reasons, explanations and evidence.

2. Look at how the mark schemes work

All your answers on the exam paper will be marked by using a level of response mark scheme. In the low tariff questions (2–4 marks) there will normally be two levels, for the medium tariff questions (5–7 marks) there will be three levels and for the higher tariff questions (8–10 marks) there will be four levels. The more detailed, informed and well reasoned your answer is, the higher up the level of responses you will advance.

A typical level of response mark scheme will look like this:

Level 1: Generalised points, not fully focused upon the topic area being examined; the general points will not be supported by accurate or relevant factual details or examples.

Answers at this level will be very simplistic and contain little factual support.

Level 2: A number of relevant points with some focus upon the question; these points will be supported by accurate factual detail, although the range might be narrow or some points might not be fully developed.

Answers will display good focus, will be supported with relevant detail and demonstrate an argument which goes some way to answering the question.

Level 3: A range of relevant points which clearly address the question and show understanding of the most important factors involved; a clear explanation which is well structured and supported by detailed and accurate factual information.

Answers at this level will be thorough and detailed; they will clearly engage with the question and provide a balanced and reasoned argument that reaches a well-supported judgement.

Guide to the WJEC GCSE History examination

You will be examined on Units 1, 2 and 3. Unit 4 is the controlled assessment unit which will be completed in class under the supervision of your history teacher and is not covered in this book.

How the WJEC GCSE History specification is organised

Unit	Unit type	Examination	Mark weighting
Unit 1	A Study in Depth	1 hour 15 minutes	50 marks
Unit 2	A Study in Depth **or** A Thematic Study	1 hour 15 minutes	50 marks
Unit 3	An Outline Study **or** A Development Study	1 hour 15 minutes	50 marks
Unit 4	Controlled Assessment – an investigation into an issue of historical debate or controversy	No exam – completed in class under controlled conditions	50 marks

This book covers the Depth Studies relating to **Russia**, **The USA** and **Germany** and the Development Study for **The USA**. It does not cover any Thematic Studies or Outline Studies.

Units 1 and 2

The examinations for Units 1 and 2 will test your knowledge and understanding of the key developments in each of the three sections for the Depth Study or Thematic Study you have studied. You will have to answer three sections, each testing particular skills.

Section A – Source evaluation

You must answer all the questions in this section.

- **Question 1(a)** is worth **2 marks** and asks you to select information from a visual source:

  a) What does Source A show you about ...?

  - Pick out at least two details from the source that are relevant to the question.
  - Make use of the information provided in the caption.
  - Do not bring in any additional factual knowledge as this will not gain you any extra marks.

- **Question 1(b)** is worth **4 marks** and asks you to explain a source and place it within its historical context by using your own knowledge:

  b) Use the information in Source B and your own knowledge to explain why ...

  - Pick out at least two details from the source and explain them in your own words.
  - You must demonstrate your knowledge of this topic by providing at least one additional factor that is not mentioned in the source.

- **Question 1(c)** is worth **5 marks** and asks you to analyse a source and make a judgement on the extent to which it supports a view:

  c) How far does Source C support the view that ...?

  - Pick out a range of relevant details from both the source and the caption, explaining them in your own words.
  - Bring in your own knowledge to expand on the details from the source and to provide additional material.
  - Give a reasoned judgement which addresses the question.

- **Question 1(d)** is worth **6 marks** and asks you to decide how useful a source is to a historian:

  d) How useful is Source D to a historian studying ...?

  - Look at the content, origin and purpose of the source:
    - Content – What does the source say?
    - Origin – Who said it? When did they say it?
    - Purpose – Why was it said? Who was it said to and why? Is it biased?
  - Make reference to the usefulness of the source to the historian – what are the limitations? Has any important information been left out?
  - Remember that a source can be useful even if it is not reliable; think about what it might be useful for.

Question 1(e) is worth **8 marks** and requires you to cross-reference two sources to look at their differing views about a historical issue:

e) Why do Sources E and F have different views about ...?

– You must comment on both sources, in each case making reference to the content and the author.

– Think about how the sources fit into your knowledge of this period; is there anything missing?

– Explain why the two sources have different views.

Section B – Knowledge and understanding

You must answer all the questions in this section.

- **Question 2(a)** is worth **4 marks** and tests your knowledge and understanding of key features:

  a) Describe the ...

  – You will need to describe at least two key features.

  – Only include information that is directly relevant.

  – Be specific; avoid generalised comments.

- **Question 2(b)** is worth **5 marks** and asks you to explain why something happened during this period.

  b) Explain why ...

  – Remember to give a variety of reasons which are well explained.

  – Give specific details such as names, dates, events, organisations and activities.

  – Always support your statements with examples.

  – Make sure the information you include is directly relevant and answers the question.

- **Question 2(c)** is worth **6 marks** and asks you to evaluate why a person, event or development was significant or important.

  c) How important was ...?

  – Remember to evaluate the importance or significance of the named individual, event or issue.

  – This question requires you to provide a judgement giving specific reasons to support your answer.

Section C – Essay writing

You must answer the essay question which is set.

- **Question 3** is worth **10 marks**, with **3 additional marks** for Spelling, Punctuation and Grammar (SPaG).

  Did ... succeed in ...?

  Was ... the most important reason/ development ...?

  – You need to develop a two-sided answer: discuss the key feature mentioned in the question and follow this by discussing other important factors.

  – Avoid generalised comments: give specific detail and ensure that you cover a range of factors/ key issues.

  – Remember the rules of essay writing: ensure your answer has an introduction, several paragraphs of discussion and a reasoned conclusion which provides a judgement upon the question set.

Unit 3

Section A – Knowledge and understanding

Three questions will appear in Section A – you have to answer **two.** They will each follow the same format of questions:

- **Question 1(a)** is worth **2 marks** and asks you to explain the message or messages from a visual source:

  a) What does Source A show you about ...?

  – Pick out at least two details from the source that are relevant to the question.

  – Make use of the information provided in the caption.

  – Do not bring in any additional factual knowledge as this will not gain you any extra marks.

- **Question 1(b)** is worth **4 marks** and tests your knowledge and understanding of key features:

  b) Describe the ...

  – You will need to describe at least two key features.

  – Only include information that is directly relevant.

  – Be specific; avoid generalised comments.

- **Question 1(c)** is worth **6 marks** and you are asked to identify change or lack of change, using your own knowledge to place each source into context:

  c) Use Sources B and C and your own knowledge to explain why … had changed.

  – You must use the information in both sources and the captions attached to them, as well as your own knowledge.

  – Cross-reference the sources, pointing out what is the same or what is different.

  – Make sure you focus on the key issue of change or lack of change.

- **Question 1(d)** is worth **8 marks** and asks you to evaluate importance or success.

  d) How important/successful was …?

  – Remember to evaluate the importance, significance or success of the named individual, event or issue.

  – This question requires you to provide a judgement giving specific reasons to support your answer.

Section B – Essay writing

You will be required to answer **one** essay question from a choice of three: questions 4, 5 or 6.

How far had … changed/improved between 1929 and 2000?

How important was … during the period 1929–2000?

How much did … change … between 1929 and 2000?

– You must include information from across the whole time period, 1929–2000. Do not spend too long on one time period, e.g. the 1960s.

– You must show how things have changed or stayed the same, remembering that some time periods will show a faster pace of change than others – make sure you explain the reasons for this.

– Remember the rules of essay writing: ensure your answer has an introduction, several paragraphs of discussion and a reasoned conclusion which provides a judgement upon the question set.

Section 1 Russia in transition, 1914–1924

Chapter 1 The causes and impact of the Russian revolutions of 1917

Key issues

You will need to demonstrate good knowledge and understanding of the key issues of this period. These are:

- What were the causes of the revolutions of 1917?
- What were the main developments during the Bolshevik seizure of power?
- What were the consequences of the revolutions of 1917?

1.1 What were the causes of the revolutions of 1917?

Russia in 1914

Revised

In 1914 Russia was ruled by Tsar Nicholas II who had absolute power. It was a vast country which covered one-sixth of the world's surface. This made it difficult to rule and Nicholas faced increasing political, economic and social problems. Russia's entry in the First World War made these problems worse.

Key terms

Autocracy – rule by one person who has complete power

Okhrana – the Tsar's secret police

Main features of Russian politics, economy and society

Difficult to govern
Russia was a vast country and its population of 130 million was made up of over 20 different ethnic groups.

Power of the Tsar
Russia was an **autocracy**. All power was in the hands of the Tsar. The **Okhrana** suppressed all opposition.

Emerging economy
Agriculture – backward farming methods resulted in low crop yields.
Industry – Russia was undergoing industrialisation but undeveloped roads and railways hindered growth.

Power of the Orthodox Church
The Church was wealthy and conservative. It exercised a powerful influence in Russian society. It supported the Tsar.

Divided society
Russian society was divided by a rigid class system:

Aristocracy (rich landowners) – comprised 1 per cent of the population but owned one-quarter of all the land. They were very rich.

Middle class (e.g. bankers, merchants, factory owners) – were beginning to emerge helped by developments in industry.

Working class
– peasants accounted for 80 per cent of the population; they lived in poor conditions and had a low life expectancy.
– industrial workers: many peasants had moved to the towns to work in the new factories; they lived in over-crowded slums and worked long hours for low wages.

The growth of opposition to the rule of the Tsar

Revised

- **The character of Tsar Nicholas** – he was not a strong ruler and refused to share power, believing that he had been chosen by God to rule; he failed to realise the nature and extent of the growing opposition to Tsarist rule.
- **The influence of Rasputin** – after 1907 the Tsar and Tsarina came to rely upon a holy man, Gregory Rasputin, to help control the blood disorder that their son Alexis suffered from; the aristocracy disliked the influence Rasputin exercised over the royal family.
- **The impact of the 1905 revolution** – the events of **Bloody Sunday** in January 1905 forced the Tsar to issue the **October Manifesto** which promised freedom of speech, an end to censorship and the calling of a **Duma**; Nicholas failed to heed the warnings of discontent and, helped by Stolypin, he reversed the October Manifesto and introduced a harsh policy of repression.
- **The failure of the Dumas** – Nicholas quickly took action to reduce the power of the Duma; the four Dumas elected between 1906 and 1914 had little influence, a factor that fuelled opposition.
- **Industrial unrest** – rapid industrialisation had created poor living and working conditions and resulted in a wave of strikes, one of the largest being in the Lena goldfields in 1912; strikes became more and more common before 1914.
- **Growth of political opposition** – after the 1905 revolution political parties became legal and they increasingly demanded change in the way Russia was governed. The main parties were:

Key terms

Bloody Sunday – the day in January 1905 when a group of peaceful demonstrators standing outside the Winter Palace in St Petersburg were fired upon by the Tsar's soldiers

October Manifesto – issued by Tsar Nicholas in 1905 it promised constitutional reform

Duma – a representative assembly that the Tsar consulted, but which had little power

Mensheviks – believed in a mass party in which power was spread among as many members as possible; they were prepared for gradual change

Bolsheviks – believed that a small party elite should organise and force a revolution

Socialist Revolutionaries (SRs)	Formed in 1901, they aimed to seize power by revolution and wanted the land to be taken from the wealthy landowners and given to the peasants; Alexander Kerensky eventually led the SRs.
Social Democratic Party	Formed in 1898, the party followed the teaching of Karl Marx and aimed to use a revolution to bring about a communist system of government; in 1903 the party split into two: • the ***Mensheviks***, led by Julius Martov and Leon Trotsky • the ***Bolsheviks***, led by Vladimir Lenin.
The Liberals	Mostly from the middle classes, the Liberals wanted to bring about peaceful political change; they wanted a democratic system in which the Tsar shared power with an elected Duma; after 1905 they split into two groups: • the *Octobrists*, led by Alexander Guchkov, who were moderate and were satisfied by the promises made by the Tsar in the October Manifesto • the *Constitutional Democrats (Cadets)*, led by Paul Milyukov, who wanted to push for further constitutional change.

Revision task

Make a copy of the following table. Use your knowledge of this section to explain how each of the following factors led to the growth of political opposition within Russia.

	How they contributed to the growth of political opposition within Russia
Autocratic rule of the Tsar	
Industrialisation	
Legalisation of political parties	

Russia's military experience in the First World War

Revised

In 1914 Russia entered the war on the side of Britain and France against Germany and Austria-Hungary. The war did not go well for Russia and by the end of 1916 she had suffered defeat after defeat:

- **26–29 August 1914** – Battle of Tannenberg: the Russian army was overwhelmed by German forces; 70,000 soldiers were killed and wounded, 50,000 taken prisoner.
- **5–9 September 1914** – Battle of Masurian Lakes: German army defeated the Russian forces; 100,000 Russians killed or wounded.
- **May 1915** – joint Austro-German forces pushed the Russians back and by the end of 1915, Germany and Austria-Hungary controlled 13 per cent of the Russian population (16 million people).
- **August 1915** – Tsar Nicholas moved to the front line to take personal command of Russian forces.
- **June 1916** – Russian counter-attack (the Brusilov Offensive) regained land lost in 1915.
- **Winter 1916–17** – the Germans were able to stop the advance and push the Russians back; all gains from the Brusilov Offensive were lost.

Why did Russia suffer so many defeats?

Revised

The main reasons were:

- **poor leadership of the generals:** they were overconfident, proved to be incompetent and used outdated tactics
- **poor leadership of the Tsar:** he lacked military experience and was blamed for the many defeats
- **weak infrastructure:** poor roads and an inadequate railway system meant that essential supplies could not reach the front line
- **a lack of supplies and equipment:** many soldiers had to share weapons and they were short of bullets, boots, winter coats and medical supplies.

The effects of the war upon Russia

Revised

- Continued news of military defeats and hardship at the front lowered morale and caused increasing numbers of soldiers to desert.
- The Russian economy was badly affected; inflation rose sharply; there was a shortage of peasants to work the land and workers to staff the factories; production levels fell and resulted in shortages of food and fuel; rationing only added to the growing discontent.
- The severe winter of 1916–17 caused further hardship with temperatures falling below –30°C.
- The decision of the Tsar to move to the front and leave the running of the country in the hands of his wife, the Tsarina Alexandra, only increased opposition to the royal family; she dismissed capable ministers and refused to accept the advice of the Duma; her increasing reliance upon Rasputin for guidance together with her German background made her more and more unpopular.

- There was growing social misery in the towns and cities due to low wages and rising prices; a poor transport system worsened food and fuel shortages; discontent was mounting.
- The murder of Rasputin in December 1916 did not end the discontent and support for the Tsar continued to diminish.
- By the end of 1916 Russia was in a chaotic state; in Petrograd there were strikes and people began to demand food.

Revision task

'Russia's poor performance in the First World War was the reason for growing unrest across the country.' How far do you agree with this statement? Copy and complete the table below:

Arguments in favour	Arguments against

Exam practice

Source A: A cartoon of 1917 showing Tsar Nicholas and Tsarina Alexandra sitting on the knee of Gregory Rasputin

What does Source A show you about the influence of Rasputin over the Russian royal family? **[2 marks]**

Answers online

Examiner's tip

In this type of question you need to look into the picture and pick out relevant details. You should also make use of what is said in the caption. Aim to write two sentences. In this instance you should mention how Rasputin is made to look bigger and more powerful than the royal family, who he appears to be controlling. It is important that you *'say what you see'*.

1.2 What were the main developments during the Bolshevik seizure of power?

Why did revolution break out in February 1917 and what were the main events?

Revised

The effects of the First World War (see pages 13–14) led to the outbreak of revolution in February 1917. The action centred upon **Petrograd** where strikes in early 1917 led to huge numbers of people taking to the streets demanding an end to food shortages, improved wages and better conditions.

- On 18 February a strike began at the Putilov steelworks.
- On 23 February, International Women's Day, large numbers of women joined about 100,000 strikers on the streets of Petrograd to protest about the queues for food.
- By 25 February there were strikes all over Petrograd with over 300,000 demonstrators on the streets.
- On 26 February Tsar Nicholas instructed the army to restore order; some shots were fired on the demonstrators.
- On 27 February soldiers in Petrograd mutinied; this signalled a turning point as up to this point the army had remained loyal to the Tsar; Nicholas ordered the Duma to dissolve but 12 members refused and set up a 'Provisional Committee'; one of them, Alexander Kerensky, demanded that Nicholas **abdicate**.
- Workers began to form councils (**soviets**) and on 27 February the first meeting of the re-formed Petrograd Soviet of Soldiers' Sailors' and Workers' Deputies was held.
- On 1 March the Petrograd Soviet issued Order Number One which took power from army officers and transferred it to the elected representatives of the soldiers.
- On 2 March Nicholas decided to return to Petrograd and was met at Pskov; his generals advised him to abdicate, which he did.
- On 3 March the Provisional Committee renamed itself the Provisional Government and became responsible for running the country, along with the Petrograd Soviet.

Key terms

Petrograd – St Petersburg sounded too German and was changed to Petrograd in 1914

Abdicate – to give up the throne

Soviet – an elected council of workers

Examiner's tip

For the 'how useful' questions such as the exam practice question below, you need to make sure that your answers include reference to what the source actually says (its **Content**), that you identify who said this (its **Origin**) and that you refer to the circumstances under which it was written (its **Purpose**). This will enable you to make a judgement about whether the information is balanced or biased and if it is biased, why it is biased. Think: **COP**.

Exam practice

Source B: A telegram sent by the President of the Duma, Michael Rodzianko, to the Tsar on 26 February 1917

'The situation is serious. The capital is in a state of anarchy. The government is paralysed; the transport system is broken down; the food and fuel supplies are completely disorganised. Discontent is general and on the increase. There is wild shooting on the streets; troops are firing at each other. It is urgent that someone enjoying the confidence of the country be entrusted with the formation of a new government. There can be no delay. Any hesitation is fatal.'

How useful is Source B to a historian studying the reasons why revolution broke out in Russia in February 1917? Explain your answer using the source and your own knowledge. **[6 marks]**

Answers online

Dual Power – the rivalry between the Provisional Government and the Petrograd Soviet

Revised

Between February and October 1917 there were two competing bodies claiming to rule Russia – the Provisional Government and the Petrograd Soviet. Their attempt to rule Russia together is referred to as the period of **Dual Power**.

The Provisional Government was made up of middle-class politicians headed by Prince Lvov. They did attempt to introduce some reforms:

- The release of political prisoners and allowing the return to Russia of political exiles.
- The introduction of freedom of speech and freedom of religion.
- The introduction of an 8-hour day for industrial workers.
- The abolition of the hated Okhrana.
- The promise of an elected parliament and universal suffrage.

Despite these reforms the Provisional Government was unpopular, and real power increasingly lay with the Petrograd Soviet which had over 3000 elected members. To begin with, the two bodies were able to work together but tension grew between them over two key issues. The first was the Provisional Government's wish to continue with the war despite the failure of the June offensive which saw the deaths of 60,000 Russian soldiers and yet more desertions. The second area of disagreement was land ownership. The peasants wanted to own all the land they farmed, taking it from the nobles and the Church. The Provisional Government did not want this.

By the autumn of 1917 it was said that the Provisional Government had '*the authority without power*' while the Petrograd Soviet had '*the power without authority*'.

Key term

Dual Power – the attempt at sharing power between the Provisional Government and the Petrograd Soviet, February–October 1917

Revision tasks

1. Write a list of the key features of the Provisional Government.
2. Now write a list of the key features of the Petrograd Soviet.
3. Compare your two lists. Make notes to show what the differences are between them.

The key events between April and September 1917

Revised

Return of Lenin

On 3 April Lenin returned from exile in Switzerland, arriving at the Finland Rail Station. On 4 April he issued his *April Theses.* He called for an end to the war with Germany; all land must be given to the peasants; all banks, factories and transport must be nationalised; the soviets should work together to form a new working-class government, pushing out the middle-class Provisional Government. Lenin used the slogans 'Peace, Bread and Land' and 'All power to the soviets'. The Bolsheviks were growing in popularity and had their own armed force – the Red Guard.

The July Days

By July the sharing of Dual Power was causing increasing strain. The war was going badly for Russia and deserting soldiers fled back to Petrograd. They joined with the Kronstadt sailors and the Bolsheviks to demand an end to the Provisional Government. For three days they rioted in Petrograd. Kerensky, Minister of War, used loyal troops to quash the rebels. Over 400 were killed or wounded. Lenin was forced to flee to exile in Finland. Kerensky now replaced Prince Lvov as Prime Minister.

The Kornilov Revolt

In September General Kornilov, Commander-in-Chief of the armed forces, attempted a ***coup d'état*** and marched his army upon Petrograd. Kerensky had no army to defend the capital and was forced to arm the Bolshevik Red Guards. Trotsky organised the Bolshevik forces which prevented Kornilov's army from entering Petrograd. They saved the Provisional Government but now refused to hand back their weapons.

Key term

Coup d'état – violent or illegal change of government

Revision tasks

1. Put together a timeline to show the key developments that occurred within Russia between February and September 1917.
2. Make a copy of the following table. Use the information in this section to explain how each of the following weakened the Provisional Government.

	How it weakened the Provisional Government
Petrograd Soviet	
Return of Lenin	
July Days	
Kornilov Revolt	

The Bolshevik seizure of power in October 1917

Revised

In February 1917 the Bolshevik Party had 24,000 members. By October this had grown to 340,000 members. In May Trotsky returned to Russia from exile, split with the Mensheviks and joined the Bolsheviks. In September he became Chairman of the Petrograd Soviet and head of the Military Revolutionary Committee. He was to play a leading role in the events of the seizure of power:

7 October	Lenin returned to Petrograd from Finland.
10 October	Lenin persuaded the Bolshevik Central Committee to agree to an uprising.
23 October	Hearing rumours of a plot, Kerensky closed down the Bolshevik papers (*Pravda* and *Izvestiya*) and attempted to round up leading Bolsheviks; Lenin ordered the revolution to begin.
Night of 24–25 October	Red Guards took control of key points in Petrograd – e.g. telegraph offices, railway stations; the battleship *Aurora* sailed up the river Neva and fired on the Winter Palace; the Red Guards stormed the Palace; several members of the government were arrested; the Provisional Government had collapsed.
26 October	Lenin announced a new all-Bolshevik government – the 'Council of People's Commissars'.

Why were the Bolsheviks successful in October 1917?

Revised

Reasons for Bolshevik success

Weakness of the Provisional Government
The Provisional Government was only a temporary body with limited power. Unlike its rival, the Petrograd Soviet, it had not been elected. Its decision to continue the war was unpopular and during the Kornilov Plot it had been forced to arm the Red Guards to protect itself. During the period of Dual Power it had to share power with the Petrograd Soviet and was the weaker partner.

Leadership of Lenin
Lenin was a gifted public speaker who used simple slogans to win support. He told people what they wanted to hear – plans for an end to the war and the re-distribution of land. He insisted on seizing power in October against opposition from other members of the party.

Lack of alternatives
The other political parties lacked clear leadership. Many were unpopular because they wanted to continue the war.

Role of Trotsky
Trotsky was an efficient organiser who directed the seizure of power from the Smolny Institute. He commanded the Red Guards and ran the Military Revolutionary Committee. He persuaded some of the soldiers in the Petrograd garrison to take part in seizing control of the city.

Revision task

Make a copy of the following table. Use the information in this section to explain the importance of each of the following in the Bolshevik seizure of power in October 1917.

	Importance
Role of Lenin	
Organisation of Trotsky	
Storming of the Winter Palace	
Unpopularity of the Provisional Government	

1.3 What were the consequences of the revolutions of 1917?

The establishment of a new Communist state

The work of the Sovnarkom

Revised

In the weeks following the Bolshevik takeover, soviets throughout Russia took control of most towns and cities. However, not all the soviets were run by Bolsheviks. Out in the countryside, the SRs (see page 12) were much more popular. In November 1917, elections for a new **Constituent Assembly** saw the SRs win 370 seats, while the Bolsheviks gained only 175 seats. When the Constituent Assembly met for the first time in January 1918 Lenin sent in his troops to dissolve it after just one day, thereby eliminating opposition to Bolshevik rule.

Key term

Constituent Assembly – a parliament elected in November 1917 to draw up a new constitution for Russia. It met only once in January 1918

Real power at this time lay with the **Sovnarkom**, a temporary Council of People's Commissioners. All the officers were Bolsheviks – Lenin was Chairman, Trotsky was Commissioner for War and Stalin was Commissioner for Nationalities.

During November and December 1917 the Sovnarkom passed a series of decrees which laid the foundations of new Bolshevik Russia:

Key terms

Sovnarkom – the Council of People's Commissars or the government of Russia

Cheka – the Bolshevik secret police

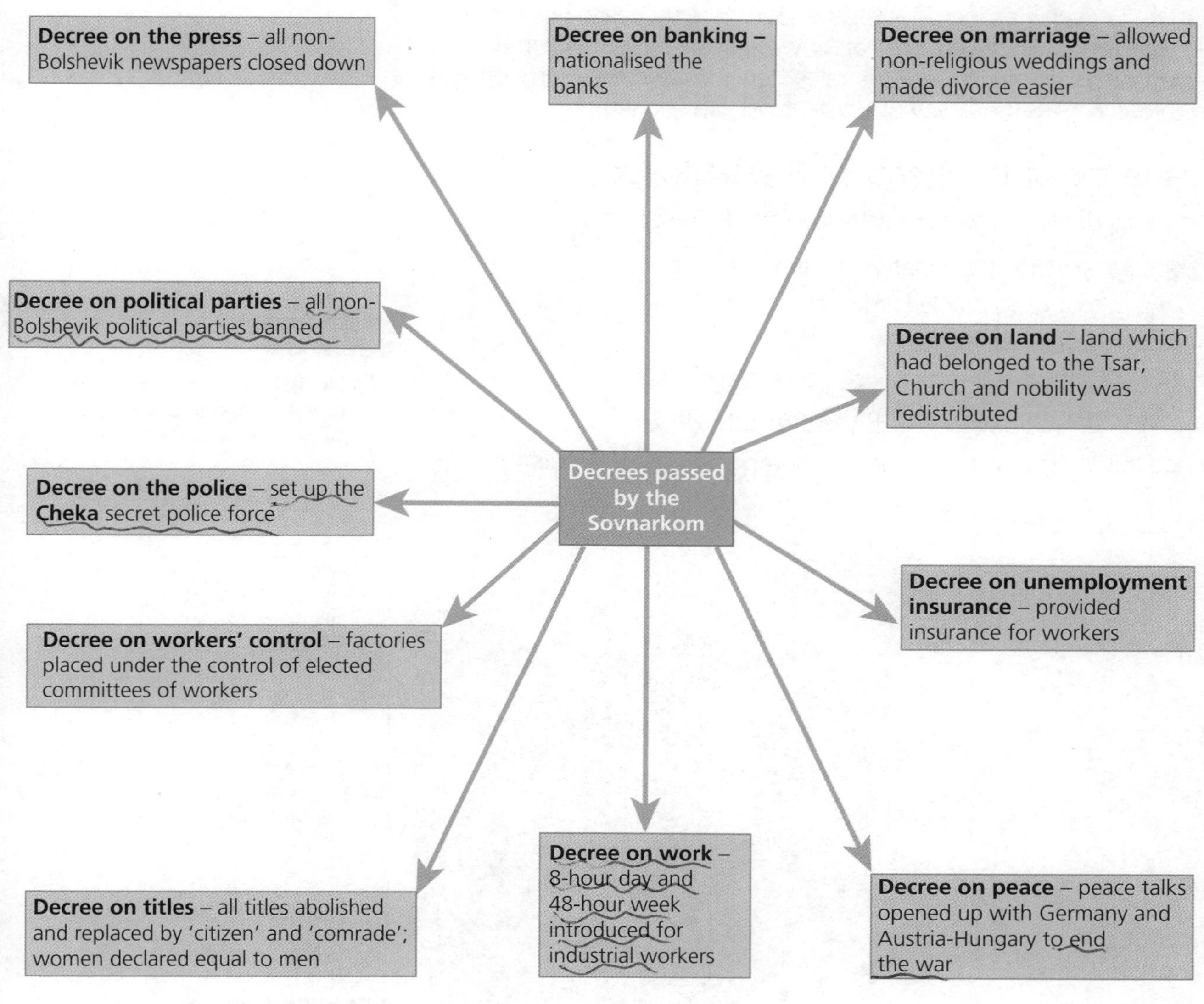

The creation of the Cheka

Revised

In December 1917 Lenin set up the 'All Russian Extraordinary Commission for Combating Counter-Revolution and Sabotage' or Cheka. This was a secret police force run by Felix Dzerzhinsky from his headquarters in the Lubyanka in Moscow. By 1921 it had 30,000 officers who were used to seek out and remove opponents of the Bolshevik regime.

Exam practice

Describe the key reforms passed by the Sovnarkom during November and December 1917. **[4 marks]**

Answers online

Examiner's tip

In 'describe' questions you need to demonstrate specific knowledge, covering 2–3 key factors. In this instance you need to name a number of specific reforms passed by the Sovnarkom and describe their key features in detail.

The steps taken to end Russia's involvement in the First World War

Revised

Lenin's decision to withdraw Russia from the war

In order to stabilise conditions within Russia and consolidate Bolshevik rule, Lenin needed to take Russia out of the war. In December 1917 Trotsky, as Commissioner for War, was sent to hold peace talks with the Germans at Brest-Litovsk. Trotsky was appalled by the German demands and wanted to end the talks. Lenin insisted they carry on and on 3 March 1918 the Treaty of Brest-Litovsk was signed.

The terms of the Treaty of Brest-Litovsk

The terms of the treaty were extremely harsh. Russia lost:

- one million square kilometres of land (see map)
- 27 per cent of its arable land
- 26 per cent of its railways
- 74 per cent of its iron ore and coal reserves
- 26 per cent of its population (50 million people).

In addition, Russia had to agree to pay **reparations** of 3 billion roubles.

Key term

Reparations – sum of money paid by a defeated power after the war as compensation

↑ **Impact of the Treaty of Brest-Litovsk**

Revision task

Write notes under the following headings to show how the Treaty of Brest-Litovsk affected Russia.

- Territory
- Transport
- Economy
- Natural resources

Chapter 2 The causes and impact of the Civil War, 1918–1921

Key issues

You will need to demonstrate good knowledge and understanding of the key issues of this period. These are:

- What were the principal causes of the Civil War?
- Who were the main sides in the Civil War?
- Why were the Reds able to win the Civil War?

2.1 What were the principal causes of the Civil War?

Growing economic and social hardship

Revised

The Bolsheviks failed to deal with the food shortages and starvation which continued in the months after the end of the war. The railway system had virtually collapsed which made transportation of foodstuffs to the cities difficult. Inflation caused prices to rise, and Russia's main wheat-supply area, the Ukraine, had been taken away by the peace treaty of Brest-Litovsk. By March 1918 the bread ration in Petrograd reached its lowest ever allocation. Such hardships led to growing violence on the streets.

Opposition to the Bolsheviks

Revised

The decision by Lenin to dissolve the Constituent Assembly in January 1918 was very unpopular with the other political parties, especially the Socialist Revolutionaries who held the majority of seats in the Assembly. The terms of the Treaty of Brest-Litovsk were very unpopular with many Russians blaming Bolsheviks for the humiliating and harsh terms. They claimed the Bolsheviks had sacrificed the national interest in order to secure peace at any price.

In May 1918 the Socialist Revolutionaries attempted a failed takeover of power. They sponsored terrorist activities and during July and August 1918 there were two unsuccessful assassination attempts against Lenin.

The rival factions who opposed the Bolsheviks

Revised

By May 1918 when Civil War erupted, a number of different factions had emerged, each with differing aims and support.

- **Czech Legion**: this was made up of 42,000 Czech soldiers who had fought on the Russian side in the war in order to gain independence from Austria-Hungary. As they were being moved across Russia by train along the Trans-Siberian railway to Vladivostok they clashed with Bolshevik forces. After a skirmish at Cheliabinsk railway station the Czech Legion rebelled and took over vital sections of the Trans-Siberian railway. This encouraged the Whites (see page 22) who now came out openly against the Bolshevik regime. This led to the start of the Civil War.

- **The Whites**: this was a mixed group that included Tsarists – nationalists, nobles, landowners and wealthy industrialists who wanted the restoration of the Tsar; the Kerenskyists (the Socialist Revolutionaries and Cadets) who wanted to see the return of the Constituent Assembly; and moderate socialists who wanted to see the Bolsheviks defeated and law and order re-established.
- **The Greens**: these were groups who refused to be conscripted into the official White armies; they included peasant armies (mostly deserters) and nationalist minorities such as the Georgian and Ukrainian armies which desired independence for their regions.
- **Foreign powers**: Britain, France, the USA and Japan all feared the spread of communism and so gave their support to the Whites; they were angry that Lenin had withdrawn Russia from the war thereby closing the Eastern Front, and that the Bolsheviks had cancelled the repaying of all loans given by the Allies to Russia.

Revision task

In your own words, write down the reasons why these different groups joined the fight against the Bolsheviks in the Civil War:

- Czech Legion
- Whites
- Greens
- Foreign powers

2.2 Who were the main sides in the Civil War?

The two main sides in the Civil War were the Reds (supporters of the Bolsheviks) and the Whites (those who opposed the Bolsheviks). The war lasted from 1918 to 1921 and resulted in victory for the Reds.

The part played by the White generals in the Civil War

Revised

To begin with the Civil War did not go well for the Reds who were attacked on all sides by White armies. (See map.)

The North: General Miller aided by British forces attempted to push south from Archangel but was unsuccessful in breaking through Red forces. Following the withdrawal of British forces from the region in the summer of 1919, Miller was eventually forced to evacuate his army to Norway in February 1920.

The West: General Yudenich's army of 15,000 reached the outskirts of Petrograd in October 1919 but failed to take the city; the Estonian troops that fought alongside him made a separate peace with the Bolsheviks and withdrew, leaving Yudenich's forces too weak to crush the Reds and in mid-1920 the army was dissolved.

The South: General Denikin's army of 150,000 men (which included a large number of Cossacks) failed in achieving its target of capturing Moscow, being driven back by Red forces led by Trotsky; in 1919 Denikin was replaced by General Wrangel but he was unable to stem the Red counter-attacks and by the end of 1920 his army had withdrawn from the Crimean Peninsula.

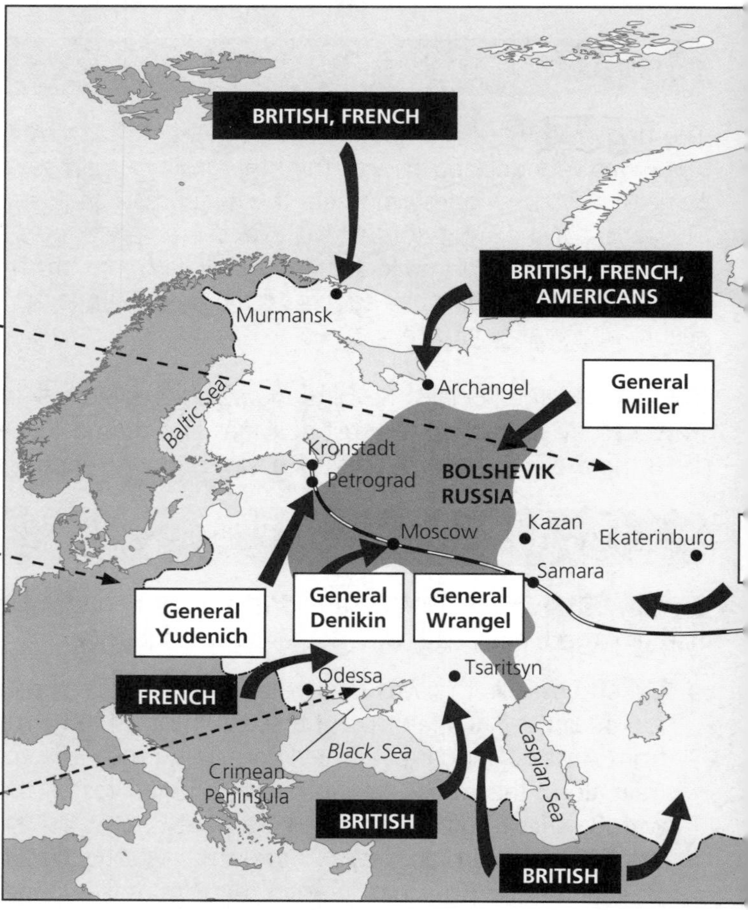

The part played by foreign powers in the Civil War

- **Britain** – was anxious to stop the spread of Bolshevism and sent the North Russian Expeditionary Force to occupy Archangel and Murmansk; British warships were sent to the Baltic and to the Black Sea to help British forces fighting in these regions.
- **France** – was very anti-Bolshevik; France established a naval base in the Black Sea port of Odessa and sent troops into the Ukraine; however, by April 1919 they had withdrawn their forces.
- **Japan** – hoping for territorial gain, the Japanese sent a sizable force into Siberia, especially the area around Vladivostok; they held the port until November 1922.
- **USA** – the US sent troops to Siberia with the aim of curtailing Japanese expansion, and also troops to Archangel to reinforce British and French forces.

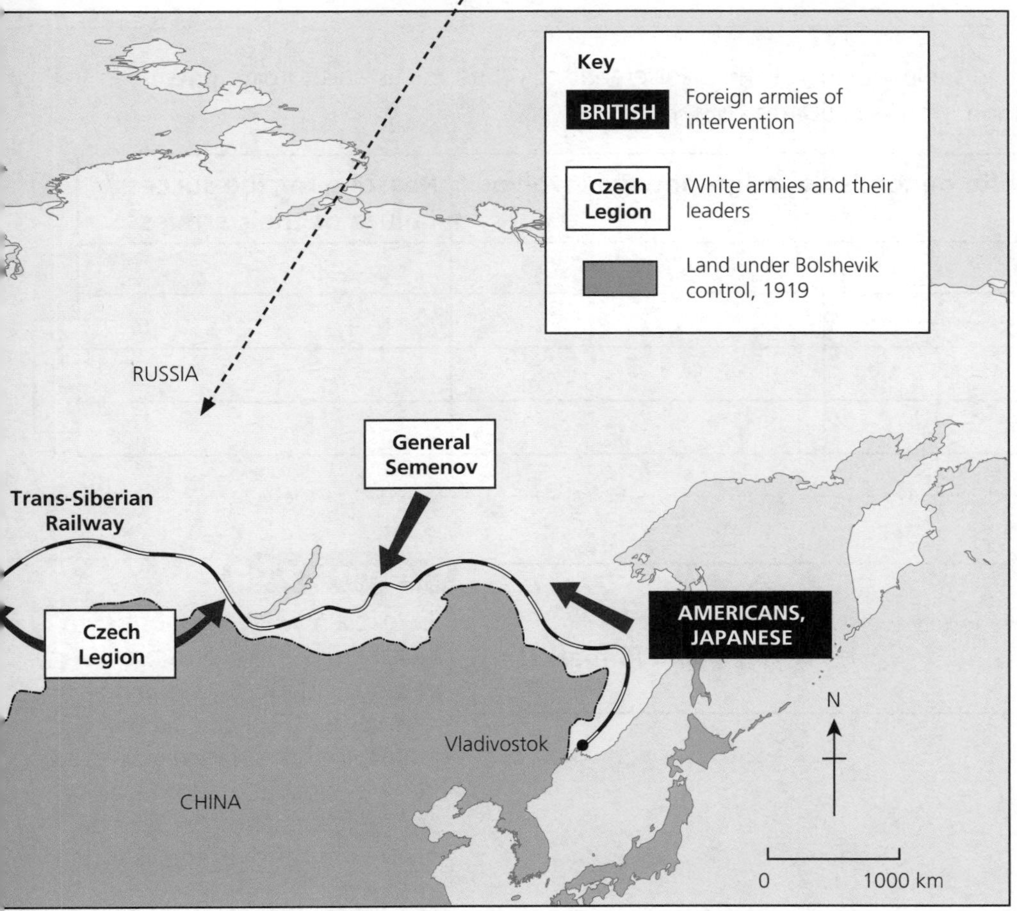

↑ **The Civil War**

The role of the Red Army in the Civil War

Revised

In contrast to the Whites, the Reds had one commander – Trotsky, and one army – the Red Army. In 1919 it numbered 3 million men and by 1920 this had grown to 5 million. However, many of the peasants were reluctant conscripts and desertions were common. In the later stages of the war the army was poorly equipped in terms of ammunition and uniforms, but generally well supplied with food due to **War Communism**. The Reds had the advantage of controlling central Russia and had command of the railways to enable it to move troops quickly.

Key term

War Communism – state control of industry and agriculture

The backbone of the Red Army was the leadership of Trotsky. He travelled to the front lines giving morale-boosting speeches. He brought back conscription, used former tsarist officers, promoted talent and introduced a harsh code of discipline.

The fate of the Tsar and his family

Revised

After the February Revolution the royal family were held under house-arrest at the palace of Tsarskoye Selo outside Petrograd. From there they were moved to Tobolsk in Siberia. In April 1918 the Bolsheviks moved them to Ekaterinburg in the Ural Mountains. By early July 1918 the Czech Legion was approaching Ekaterinburg and, fearing the royal family would be rescued and handed over to the Whites, Lenin ordered their execution. At 2a.m. on 17 July the Tsar and his family were shot and killed in the basement of Ipatiev House. The bodies were buried in a forest on the outskirts of the town and remained undiscovered until 1991.

Revision task

Make a copy of the following table looking at the involvement of White forces and foreign powers in the Civil War. Use the information in this section to complete it.

	Names of White generals	Foreign powers involved	Reasons for the success/ failure of their armies
North			
South			
East			
West			

Exam practice

Explain why the Tsar and his family were murdered in 1918. **[5 marks]**

Answers online

Examiner's tip

In 'explain why' questions you need to give two or more reasons, supporting your answer with specific factual detail. In this instance you need to talk about the approaching White forces and the decision by Lenin not to let the Tsar be rescued.

2.3 Why were the Reds able to win the Civil War?

The Reds were able to win the Civil War because of a combination of their own strengths and, equally important, the weaknesses of their enemies.

The strengths of the Reds

Revised

	The strengths of the Reds
The leadership of Lenin and Trotsky	Lenin was an inspirational figure who provided leadership and direction. He was ruthless in introducing War Communism and in the use of the Cheka. Trotsky was the key to the success of the Red Army, providing organisational leadership, directing strategy, and inspiring his men.
Use of the Cheka	This body proved to be very efficient in rooting out opposition to the Bolsheviks. During the **Red Terror** suspected 'enemies of the state' were arrested, tortured and executed.
War Communism	To win the Civil War Lenin needed to keep the Red Army supplied with food and weapons. The state took over all aspects of the economy, nationalising major industry and controlling the production and distribution of all goods. War Communism operated between 1918 and 1921 but was especially unpopular with the peasants because the state took food from them.
Use of propaganda	The Reds had a strong cause – they were fighting to preserve the October Revolution – which helped them deliver a powerful message; they made very effective use of propaganda, especially posters and films, to paint a black picture of the Whites and the foreign powers. Propaganda trains and boats were used to explain the ideas of communism to the people.
Control of the central area and the railways	The Reds occupied central Russia, which made communications easier; they moved the capital back to Moscow which was at the heart of the railway network; control of the railway was important for the movement of troops and supplies; they controlled the main armaments factories, which were located in central areas.
Support from the peasantry	Lenin's issue of the Decree of Land (1917) helped to win peasant support; the brutality of the White armies drove many peasants to support the Bolsheviks as the lesser of two evils.

Key term

Red Terror – period of Cheka repression under the Bolsheviks

The weaknesses of the Whites

Revised

	Weaknesses of the Whites
Lack of unity	The Whites were made up of many different political parties who constantly squabbled and did not trust each other. They were not organised into a single fighting force and operated as a number of independent armies. This meant the Reds were able to deal with the White forces one at a time.
Poor leadership	The Whites lacked leaders of the quality of Lenin and Trotsky. The White generals could not agree on strategy and there were high levels of corruption and indiscipline in the White armies. White forces were responsible for much brutality which went unpunished.
Weak support from foreign powers	Foreign support proved to be half-hearted and ineffective. France had withdrawn her military support by April 1919. There was little cooperation between the foreign powers and the Bolsheviks made use of the propaganda value of presenting themselves as defenders of Russian soil against foreign forces.
Geographical spread	White forces were scattered round the edges of the central area, separated by large distances which made communications difficult. They had only limited access to the railways and their forces and supplies had to cover large distances by poor roads.
Low morale	The murder of the Tsar in July 1918 weakened the White cause and lowered morale. Their forces lacked a common cause.

Exam practice

Source A: Y Kukushkin, an official Communist historian, writing in his book *History of the USSR* (1981)

'The Communist Party, led by Lenin, sent the best of its members to join the Red Army. By the end of 1918 Lenin had sent over 1,700,000 men to fight the Whites. The Red Army was a formidable force. Even so, on every battlefront, Red Army units had to fight against an enemy who was better equipped, better trained and numerically superior. The Red Army was composed of workers and peasants who were utterly devoted to the cause of the revolution. That was what ensured their victory.'

How far does Source A support the view that the Red Army won the Civil War because it was fighting for a cause? **[5 marks]**

Answers online

Examiner's tip

In the 'how far' questions you need to give a judgement upon the accuracy of the information given in the source and its attribution. In this instance you need to pick out the strengths of the Red Army from the source, link it to your own knowledge, and comment upon the fact that the source is the opinion of a Communist author. It is therefore more likely to support the viewpoint.

Chapter 3 The development of the Communist state, 1921–1924

Key issues

You will need to demonstrate good knowledge and understanding of the key issues of this period. These are:

- Why did Lenin introduce the New Economic Policy and how successful was it?
- Did Lenin succeed in establishing a Communist state in Russia?
- What was Lenin's legacy to Russia?

3.1 Why did Lenin introduce the New Economic Policy and how successful was it?

By 1921 Russia's economy was in ruins. The years of civil war had drained the country. The strain of War Communism had added to the burden and between 1920 and 1921 a drought contributed towards a major famine. Growing opposition to Communist rule convinced Lenin that a drastic change of direction was needed.

The introduction of the New Economic Policy

Revised

Lenin introduced the **New Economic Policy** for a number of reasons:

- **The effects of War Communism** – the peasants proved reluctant to give up their produce to the state and grew less grain and bred fewer animals; this led to food shortages in 1920 followed by a major famine in 1921; between 5 and 7 million Russians starved to death during the famine.
- **Growing opposition in the countryside** – continued requisitioning resulted in hundreds of peasant uprisings across Russia, the biggest being in the Tambov region in 1921–22 which took a year to suppress.
- **Growing opposition in the cities** – industrial workers were forced to work long hours and were forbidden to strike; many fled to the countryside in search of food; Petrograd lost 70 per cent of its inhabitants and Moscow 50 per cent during the years of War Communism; in January 1921 the bread ration was cut by a third in many cities which caused outbreaks of strikes and demonstrations.
- **The Kronstadt mutiny** – in March 1921 there was a rebellion of sailors and dockyard workers at the Kronstadt naval base; they demanded better conditions for workers and an end to War Communism. Trotsky ordered General Tukhachevsky to crush the rising. It took 60,000 troops three weeks to restore order; 20,000 men were either killed or sent away to the **gulags**.

The Kronstadt rebellion shocked Lenin as these sailors had previously been loyal supporters. In March 1921 he announced the abandonment of War Communism and the introduction of the New Economic Policy.

Key terms

New Economic Policy – introduced by Lenin in 1921 to win back the support of the people, it allowed private businesses, farms and profit

Gulag – a prison where inmates were punished by forced labour

Revision task

Construct your own spider diagram to show the reasons why Lenin introduced the New Economic Policy. Place the most important reason at the top and the other reasons in a clockwise direction, according to what you think is their order of importance.

The main features of the New Economic Policy

Revised

Lenin viewed the New Economic Policy as only a temporary measure designed to allow the country to get back on its feet. It would reduce central government control of the economy and allow free enterprise.

Key terms

Nepmen – private traders

Kulak – a better-off peasant who benefited from the NEP

THE NEW ECONOMIC POLICY

- Small factories (less than 20 workers) were returned to former owners and allowed to make a profit.
- Trade with foreign countries was encouraged.
- Grain requisitioning was stopped.
- Traders could buy, sell and make goods at a profit. **Nepmen** emerged who bought goods cheaply and sold them for a profit.
- Peasants who increased their food production would pay less tax.
- Key industries such as coal and steel remained under state control, as did transport and the banking system.
- Peasants would pay a small fixed amount of grain as tax but any surplus they could sell for profit. This benefitted the **kulaks** more than the poorer peasants.
- Electrification took place through the building of a network of power stations.

Exam practice

Describe the key features of the New Economic Policy. **[4 marks]**

Answers online

Examiner's tip

Remember that in this 'describe' question you need to look at two or more key features of the NEP, supporting them with specific factual detail.

How successful was the NEP?

Revised

By 1923 the Russian economy was showing signs of considerable improvement but the introduction of the NEP had stirred up a fierce debate within the Communist Party, one bitter critic of it being Trotsky.

Achievements	Shortcomings
By 1923: • food production had increased and good harvests in 1922 and 1923 brought an end to the great famine • cereal production had increased by 23% compared to 1920 • shops, cafés and restaurants re-opened • industry began to recover, especially small-scale enterprises. Between 1920 and 1923 factory output rose by 200% • nepmen appeared and by 1923 these middle-men traders handled three-quarters of all retail trade • kulaks did well, selling their own produce and employing poorer peasants to work for them.	Critics of the NEP claimed that: • it was going against the ideals of the October Revolution and encouraging the emergence of a capitalist society • nepmen and kulaks were criticised as being greedy capitalists who had become rich upon the hard work of others • the NEP encouraged corruption and vice, especially in the cities where crime increased • it resulted in the 'scissors crisis' – a surplus of food resulted in a fall of agricultural prices while the price of industrial goods rose because they were in shorter supply • some critics said that NEP stood for 'New Exploitation of the Proletariat'.

3.2 Did Lenin succeed in establishing a Communist state in Russia?

Between 1921 and 1924 the Communists were able to spread their control over most aspects of life in Russia.

The organs of the Communist State

Revised

The Communist Party in the Soviet Union (CPSU)

In 1922 the Union of Soviet Socialist Republics (**USSR**) was set up. The Communist Party controlled the government at every level and all key positions in government were held by members of the Communist Party.

Key term

USSR – Union of Soviet Socialist Republics, the name given to Russia and its allied socialist republics after 1922. Eventually the USSR comprised 15 republics

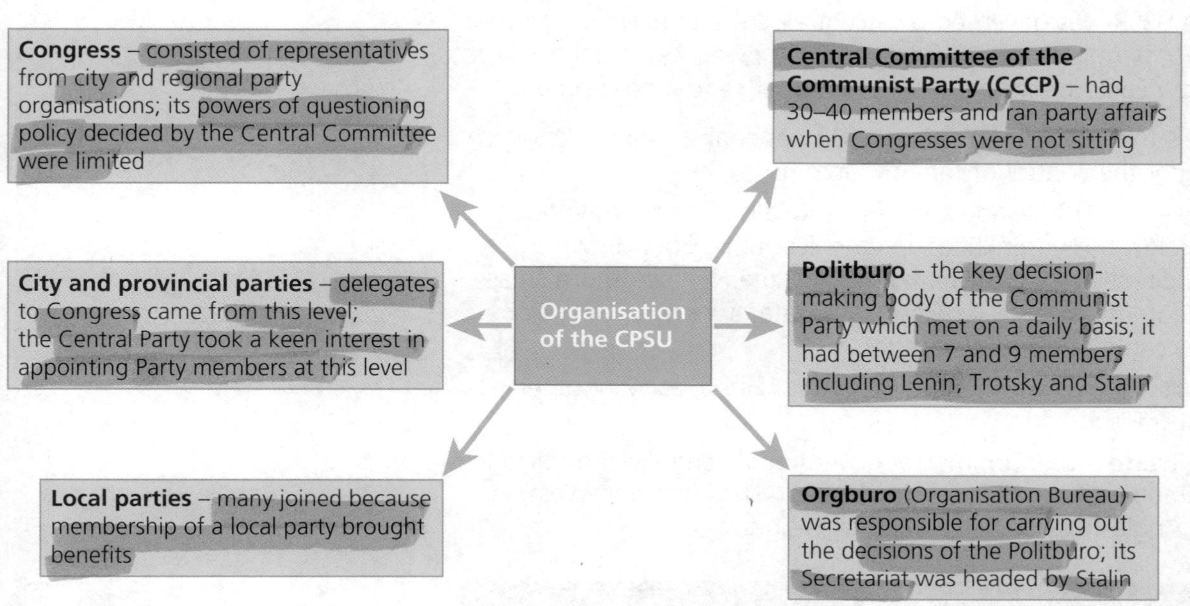

The government of the USSR

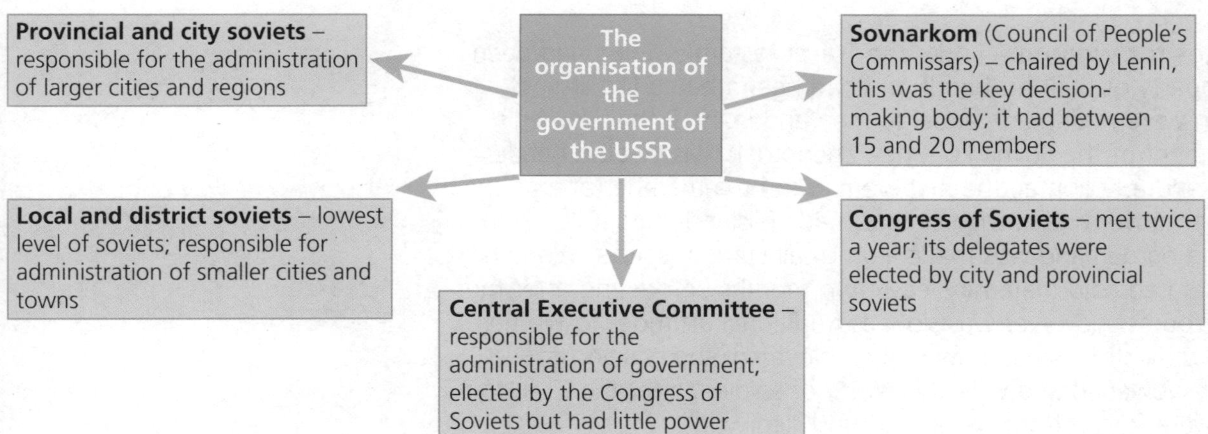

The Comintern (Communist International)

At the Tenth Party Congress in March 1919 Lenin announced the creation of the Comintern; its purpose was to organise socialist revolutions across Europe; it had limited success and did much to worsen relations with other countries, especially Britain.

The Cheka and the Red Terror

The Cheka were used ruthlessly to search out and remove any opposition to the Communist regime. Any person showing any sign of opposition was arrested and shot without trial or sent to work in the gulags; victims included priests, judges, merchants, traders, workers and peasants. During the Red Terror the Cheka killed over 200,000 people and sent 85,000 to the gulags.

Revision task

Describe the role of each of the following organisations:

1. Central Committee
2. Politburo
3. Orgburo
4. Sovnarkom
5. Comintern

The growth of centralisation

Revised

By 1924 the USSR was governed by a centralised, one-party dictatorship which did not permit anyone to challenge its power. Key aspects of the economy now came under the direct control of central government.

- **Finance** – the Decree on Banking 1917 nationalised all banks which came under the control of the Sovnarkom.
- **Industry** – in 1918 all industry was nationalised and came under the control of the Vesenkha (Supreme Economic Council) which reported directly to the Sovnarkom; while the NEP did return small factories (of less than 20 workers) to private ownership, all major industries came under state control.
- **Transport** – the railway system was nationalised, as were other means of transport.
- **Foreign trade** – the Communist government centrally controlled all foreign trade and the NEP developed trade links with the West; in 1921 an Anglo-Russian trade treaty was signed.

Life under Communist rule

Revised

Lenin attempted to impose Communist ideology over all aspects of life in Russia:

- **Changes for women** – under the Tsarist system women had been the property of their husbands and had been treated like slaves. Women were now made equal to men and in 1919 the Women's Department of the Sovnarkom (the Zhenotdel) was created headed by Alexandra Kollontai, the first woman to be a member of any European government. Divorce was made easier and in 1920 abortion on demand was made legal in all state hospitals. Women were granted paid maternity leave two months before and after the birth. Progress however was slow as traditional attitudes to women proved difficult to break down. In employment the position of women worsened and with the return of soldiers after the Civil War many were forced from skilled into unskilled work.
- **Control over education** – Lenin recognised the importance of controlling education to help spread Communist ideology. Every child was to receive nine years of free education. The curriculum was under state control with a focus upon practical education and political ideology. Youth groups were set up to indoctrinate young minds – the 'Pioneers' for those under 15 and the '**Komsomol**' for those over 15.

Key term

Komsomol – the Communist youth movement

- **Suppression of religion** – Lenin saw the Orthodox Church as a source of resistance to Communism. As many Russians were religious he realised that he could not ban religion outright so he adopted a middle way. The Decree for the Separation of the Church and State allowed people the freedom of worship but at the same time destroyed the power and wealth of the Church. All church property was seized, many monasteries were closed down, all Sunday schools were closed and the teaching of religion was banned in schools. However, there was strong resistance to these changes in many areas.
- **Cultural life** – the Communists wanted to control all aspects of culture and set up the Commissariat of Public Enlightenment. The arts were encouraged to follow a more modern style, rejecting traditional forms. Paintings had to show happy workers contributing to the victory of Communism and the dramatic events of 1917 were a very popular theme for paintings, with Lenin portrayed as the hero.
- **The use of propaganda and censorship** – censorship was imposed immediately after the October Revolution. The Decree of the Press in 1917 banned all non-Bolshevik newspapers and in 1922 pre-publication censorship was introduced on books, articles, poems and all writings. Various methods of propaganda were used to put across Communist ideology. Great use was made of posters and banners. Statues of revolutionary figures, especially Lenin, were put up. The Department of Agitation and Propaganda (**Agitprop**) was set up to organise stage plays, motion pictures and other art forms. Agitprop trains and boats toured the country. Sergei Eisenstein's films *October* and *Battleship Potemkin* portrayed the power of the people as being the decisive factor in the Bolshevik seizure of power.

Key terms

Propaganda – means of spreading political ideas, often through the use of media such as posters, film, radio and the press

Censorship – the control of what is printed and broadcast: books, newspapers, plays, films, and the suppression of anything considered to be against the state

Agitprop – abbreviation used for the Department for Agitation and Propaganda. Its function was to spread Communist ideology

Revision task

Copy and complete this chart to show the impact Communism had upon each of the following:

	The impact of Communism was ...
Women	
Education and young people	
Religion	
Cultural life	

Exam practice

How important was the use of propaganda and censorship in the establishment of a Communist state? **[6 marks]**

Answers online

Examiner's tip

In the 'how important' questions you need to identify 2–3 key reasons why something was important, using specific factual detail to back up your comments. In this instance you should refer to the use of the Agitprop trains and boats, the use of posters and films, and how important it was to control what was written and broadcast about the regime. Remember to provide a judgement on 'how important' propaganda and censorship were.

3.3 What was Lenin's legacy to Russia?

The power struggle to succeed Lenin

Revised

Lenin's declining health

In August 1918 there was a failed assassination attempt on Lenin's life, with a bullet being permanently lodged in his neck. Lenin recovered but his long working days caused him to become exhausted and after 1921 there was a sharp decline in his health. In May 1922 he suffered a stroke which paralysed the right side of his body and left him temporarily unable to speak. During his recovery the USSR was ruled by a group of three – Stalin, Zinoviev and Kamenev. All three disliked Trotsky. In December 1922 Lenin suffered a second stroke, followed by a third in March 1923. He was unable to talk and was confined to a wheelchair. He died in January 1924.

Lenin's political *Testament* – possible successors

In December 1922 Lenin dictated his political *Testament* which detailed the strengths and weaknesses of the men who might succeed him. He concluded that no one person should succeed him and instead he wanted a collective leadership.

Lenin's *Testament*	
Trotsky	Able but seen as too arrogant and self-assured
Stalin	Held too much power as General Secretary and he had been very rude to Lenin's wife. Lenin recommended that he be removed from his posts
Bukharin	Not sufficiently Marxist
Kamenev	Showed unwillingness to commit to revolution in 1917
Zinoviev	Showed unwillingness to commit to revolution in 1917

At the time of Lenin's death no decision about his successor had been made. The struggle for the leadership lasted four years and was eventually won by Joseph Stalin.

The power struggle after Lenin's death

Revised

Following Lenin's death, Stalin joined with Kamenev and Zinoviev to discredit Trotsky and block his chances of success. They also blocked the appeal by Lenin's widow to have Lenin's *Testament* published by the Central Committee. When Lenin died, Trotsky was in southern Russia and he later claimed that Stalin lied about the date of the funeral. Trotsky's failure to attend the funeral lost him support and made him look arrogant and disrespectful. Stalin played a leading part in the proceedings and was seen as the chief mourner.

In the battle to succeed Lenin two main contenders emerged – Trotsky and Stalin:

Trotsky	Stalin
• He was seen by party members as an outsider – he was a Menshevik until early 1917. • He seriously underestimated Stalin, believing him to be intellectually inferior and unambitious. • He was seen as being too big-headed, possessing a superiority complex. • He favoured 'World Revolution', wanting the USSR to support communist revolutions in other countries, a policy which was not popular.	• He used his key role as General Secretary to appoint officials who supported him and he removed supporters of Trotsky. • He crafted the image of having been close to Lenin, doctoring pictures. • He manipulated the other rivals to turn against Trotsky. • He favoured 'Socialism in one country', a policy which was popular within the Communist Party.

By the late 1920s Stalin had outmanoeuvred and expelled his rivals within the Politburo to make himself supreme leader of the USSR.

Revision task

Construct a spider diagram showing the reasons why Stalin was successful in the leadership contest. Rank the reasons in order of importance, proceeding clockwise with the most important at twelve o'clock.

Lenin's legacy

Revised

Lenin left behind a country which had gone through tremendous change in a short period of time. His legacy has been a matter of much historical debate.

Positives	Negatives
• As Party Leader, Lenin played a central role in directing affairs to secure the Bolshevik takeover of power in October 1917, over-ruling opposition within the Party. • His boundless energy and organisational power meant that he was able to restore some political, economic and social stability to the country by 1924. • He was ruthless, believing that 'the means justify the end'. He made extensive use of the Cheka to eliminate opposition and introduced War Communism to feed and supply the Red Army during the Civil War. • He was prepared to make unpopular decisions to secure the continuance of Bolshevik rule – he abandoned War Communism and introduced the NEP which was criticised by Party radicals. • He helped create a new Russia – the USSR – and a new type of Marxism called Marxism–Leninism.	• Lenin ended democracy and created a one-party state in which no opposition was allowed, there was a powerful secret police and an all-powerful political party operated at every level of government. • His introduction of the NEP was seen as an abandonment of the true ideals of Communism as it introduced elements of capitalism into the USSR. • He failed to secure the succession – he suggested a collective leadership but left no clear instructions as to how this was to be achieved. He failed to train a successor and the result was a long-drawn-out power struggle. • Some historians see the harsh nature of Stalin's regime with its purges and terror as the direct consequence of the system created by Lenin after 1917.

On Lenin's death, Winston Churchill commented: *'The Russian people's worst misfortune was his birth; their next worst – his death.'*

Exam practice

Source A: Lenin's qualities as described by the Bolshevik Party's Central Committee, January 1924

'A fearless mind, a will of iron, a burning hatred of slavery and oppression, a revolutionary passion that moved mountains, boundless faith in the creative energies of the masses, vast organisational genius.'

Source B: Part of an obituary notice printed in the British newspaper, *The Times*, 23 January 1924

'A man of iron will and inflexible ambition, Lenin had no scruple about methods and treated human beings as mere material for his purpose ... This is not the place to describe in detail the terrible achievements of Bolshevism ... the Communist experiment has brought Russia to economic ruin, famine and barbarism.'

Why do Sources A and B have different views about the qualities of Lenin as a leader? **[8 marks]**

Answers online

Examiner's tip

In this type of question you need to compare and contrast two sources, making clear reference to both the content and the authors. You need to provide a judgement about why the views differ and this can best be explained through the attributions – Source A was written by the Bolshevik Party, Source B by a British newspaper. Both offer biased viewpoints.

Chapter 4 The main political and social challenges facing America, 1910–1929

Key issues

You will need to demonstrate good knowledge and understanding of the key issues of this period. These are:

- Why did immigration become such a major issue in American society?
- Was America a country of religious and racial intolerance during this period?
- Was the 1920s a decade of organised crime and corruption?

4.1 Why did immigration become such a major issue in American society?

Today America is a multi-cultural and multi-racial society that is mainly the result of immigration. Successive waves of immigrants (40 million had arrived by 1919) resulted in a **melting pot** of different races, cultures, religions and languages.

Key term

Melting pot – a mixture of races and nationalities

Why people wished to emigrate to America

Revised

To help colonise the country, the US Government had traditionally followed an **open door policy** towards immigration which was designed to make entry into America as easy as possible. The fact that anybody could enter the country was a key attraction. Over 70 per cent of all immigrants entering the country were processed at Ellis Island, just off New York.

A combination of **push and pull factors** caused this mass immigration:

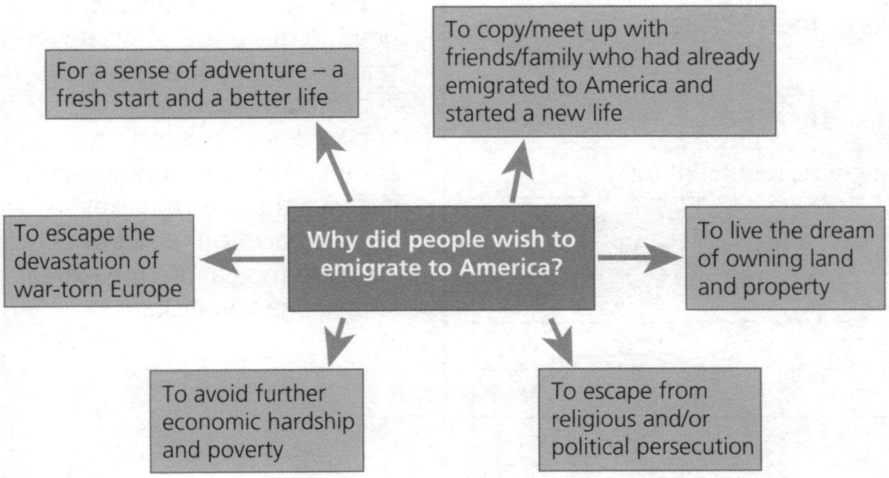

Why did people wish to emigrate to America?

- For a sense of adventure – a fresh start and a better life
- To copy/meet up with friends/family who had already emigrated to America and started a new life
- To live the dream of owning land and property
- To escape from religious and/or political persecution
- To avoid further economic hardship and poverty
- To escape the devastation of war-torn Europe

Key terms

Open door policy – free admission of immigrants

Push and pull factors – push factors are those which cause people to move *away* from an area and pull factors are those which cause people to move *to* an area. In this case, push factors are those which caused immigrants to leave their homeland and pull factors are those which attracted them to America

Revision task

Study the diagram. Make a note next to each factor to show whether it is a push or a pull factor.

The growing demand to restrict immigration

Revised

In the 1920s many Americans were starting to question the open door policy towards immigration:

- The trauma and devastation caused in Europe by the First World War meant that there was a sharp rise in the number of immigrants entering America to escape poverty and persecution.
- There was a large increase in the number of immigrants arriving from Eastern Europe (13 million between 1900 and 1914).
- Americans increasingly felt 'swamped' by the rising number of immigrants.
- Immigrants were seen to offer little – they were often poor, illiterate and could not speak English.
- The growth of **xenophobia** and the perception of an ideal citizen being a **WASP** led Americans to look down on the immigrants from Eastern Europe and Italy.
- The cultural and religious backgrounds of immigrants from Eastern Europe were different from those of many Americans and this led to fear and hatred.
- The rise of Bolshevism (Communism) in Russia following revolution in 1917 led to a fear of immigrants bringing communist ideas with them into America.

Key terms

Xenophobia – an irrational fear or hatred of foreigners

WASP – White, Anglo-Saxon, Protestant

Legislation introduced by the US Government to restrict immigration

Revised

Increasing pressure was placed upon the US Congress to pass measures to restrict entry into America. Four important measures were introduced, each one being stricter than the previous one.

Year	Measure	Key features
1917	Literacy Test	All immigrants had to pass a literacy test in English.
1921	Emergency Quota Act	This introduced a 3% quota based upon the total population of each ethnic group in 1910; it allowed 357,000 immigrants to enter each year.
1924	National Origins Act	This cut the quota to 2% based upon the 1890 census. It allowed more people from northern Europe to enter.
1929	Immigration Act	This restricted immigration to 150,000 per year. No Asians were allowed. Northern and western Europeans were allocated 85% of places.

Exam practice

Use the information in Source A and your own knowledge to explain how the immigration acts of the 1920s restricted entry into the USA. **[4 marks]**

Source A: Quota levels of immigrants to the USA

	Number of immigrants restricted to:	
	3% of the population in **1921**	2% of the population in **1924**
UK/Ireland	77,342	62,574
Germany/Austria	75,342	52,012
Eastern Europe	63,191	10,902
Italy	42,957	3,845

Answers online

Examiner's tip

In this type of question you need to make use of what is said in the source and, most importantly, use your own knowledge of this topic to add extra information. In this instance the source makes no reference to the Act of 1929, so this can be the extra knowledge you include.

The fear of political extremism entering the USA

The Red Scare

Revised

Many Americans became alarmed over events in Europe especially following the Bolshevik Revolution in Russia in 1917 which led to the set up of a communist system of government. Many feared that immigrants would spread **communist** and **anarchist** ideas into America and events during 1919–20 only added to these fears, leading to the growth in xenophobia:

- There were 3600 strikes during 1919 which added to the fear that a communist revolution was pending.
- During 1919 a bomb planted by an anarchist group badly damaged the house of the Attorney-General, Mitchell Palmer.
- In April 1919 a bomb planted in a church in Milwaukee killed ten people.
- In September 1920 an anarchist bomb exploded on Wall Street killing 38 people.

Such actions gave rise to the **Red Scare**, the fear that anarchists and communists threatened America.

Key terms

Communist – a person who believes in the ideas of Karl Marx to create a classless society with all land and business owned collectively

Anarchist – a person who wants to remove all forms of government

Red Scare – fear that immigrants from Eastern Europe were spreading communist ideas across America

The Palmer Raids

Revised

The Palmer Raids were organised by the Attorney-General, Mitchell Palmer, Head of the US Department of Justice. It was a response to the Red Scare and it involved the arrest of over 6000 suspected communists in 36 cities across America. Trade unionists, Jews, Catholics and black people were particularly targeted. These people were held for several weeks without charge and hundreds were later deported.

The Sacco and Vanzetti case

Revised

This case was important because it displayed a clear instance of racial discrimination and highlighted the unfairness of the US legal system towards immigrants.

- On 5 May 1920 two Italian immigrants – Nicola Sacco and Bartolomeo Vanzetti – were arrested and charged with carrying out a robbery at a shoe factory in Massachusetts in which two people died.
- Their trial opened in May 1921 but the case against them was not strong – 61 eyewitnesses identified the two men but the defence produced 107 witnesses who said they were elsewhere at the time of the robbery.
- The case aroused mass media attention and the judge, Webster Thayer, seemed determined to find the two men guilty.
- The jury found them guilty and they were sentenced to death; their appeal failed and they were executed by electric chair in August 1927.
- The treatment of these two anarchist immigrants typifies the hysteria of the Red Scare.

Revision tasks

1. Create your own spider diagram to show why the Red Scare occurred during the early 1920s.
2. 'Sacco and Vanzetti did not receive a fair trial.' How far do you agree with this statement? First list the arguments for the statement – that they *did not* receive a fair trial. Then list the arguments against – that they *did* receive a fair trial.

4.2 Was America a country of religious and racial intolerance during this period?

Religious fundamentalism and the Monkey Trial

Revised

The period 1910–29 saw a growing divide between the more conservative-minded rural areas and the more modern city culture of urban America. The rural areas tended to be very religious, especially those in the **Bible Belt** states of the south east such as Alabama and Tennessee. Many of the people in these states were Christian **fundamentalists** who believed that everything in the Bible had to be taken literally and must not be questioned.

- Traditional and modern America clashed over the 'Monkey Trial', which was an argument over Darwin's theory of **evolution**.
- The Bible Belt states believed in **creationism** and in 1924–25 six states banned the teaching of evolution in their schools.
- A biology teacher called John Scopes from Dayton, Tennessee, ignored the ban. He was arrested and put on trial in July 1925.
- Scopes was found guilty of teaching evolution and fined $100.
- The case was important because it showed how the fundamentalists were trying to curb the freedom of thought.

Key terms

Bible Belt – an area of southern America where Christian belief is strong

Fundamentalist – a religious person who goes to church regularly and believes in the Bible word for word

Evolution – the theory that living species have developed gradually over time, through a long series of generations

Creationism – the belief that all living species were created by God simultaneously

Exam practice

Source A: An interview with Austin Peay, Governor of the southern state of Tennessee, reported in the *Nashville Banner* newspaper on 24 March 1925

'The people have the right to regulate what is taught in their schools. Right or wrong, there is a deep, widespread belief that something is shaking the fundamentals of the country, both in religion and morals. It is the opinion of many that an abandonment of the old-fashioned faith and belief in the Bible is our trouble in a large degree. It is my own belief that the [anti-evolution] law is a popular protest against an irreligious tendency to exalt a so-called science, and deny the Bible in some schools.'

How useful is Source A to a historian studying the reasons why the Monkey Trial took place in 1925? **[6 marks]**

Answers online

Examiner's tip

For the 'how useful' questions you need to make sure that your answers include reference to what the source actually says (its **Content**), that you identify who said this (its **Origin**) and that you refer to the circumstances under which it was written (its **Purpose**). This will enable you to make a judgement about whether the information is balanced or biased and if it is biased, why it is biased. Think: **COP**.

Attitudes towards black Americans and racial minorities

The 1920s was a period which witnessed a growth in racial intolerance particularly against black Americans and Native Americans. This hostility was fuelled by a corresponding growth in membership of an extreme racist organisation called the Ku Klux Klan.

The Jim Crow laws

Revised

In 1910 some 12 million black people lived in America, 75 per cent of them in the southern states. Slavery had been abolished in the southern states in the 1860s but the white-controlled state governments soon introduced laws to control the freedom of black Americans. The **Jim Crow laws** introduced **segregation**, separating black and white Americans in schools, parks, hospitals, swimming pools, libraries and other public places. Life for black Americans living in the south was very hard. They were discriminated against and found it difficult to get fair treatment. They could not vote and were denied the right to a decent education and a good job.

Key terms

Jim Crow laws – laws which brought about segregation and discrimination against black Americans living in the southern states of America

Segregation – keeping a group separate from the rest of society, usually on the basis of race or religion

The Great Migration

Revised

Segregation did not exist in the northern states and faced with increasing racial tension in the south, many black Americans decided to migrate to the industrial cities of the north in search of a new job and a better standard of living. Between 1916 and 1920 almost 1 million people made the trek north in what became known as the 'Great Migration'. They flooded into cities like Chicago, Detroit, New York and Philadelphia.

However, life in the north was often just as difficult. Black Americans continued to be treated as second-class citizens. They were the last to be hired and the first to be fired from jobs in bad times. They received low pay and lived in poor neighbourhoods called ghettos, such as Harlem in New York. Growing racial tension resulted in the outbreak of riots in 20 US cities in 1919, the worst being in Chicago and Washington DC.

The reaction of black Americans to racial injustice

Revised

Two organisations, very different in their beliefs and methods, attempted to draw attention to the injustices faced by black Americans and fight for a better future:

The National Association for the Advancement of Coloured People (NAACP)	The Universal Negro Improvement Association (UNIA)
Founded in 1910 by William Du Bois, by 1919 it had 90,000 members in 300 branches. Du Bois believed in peaceful, non-violent protest using legal methods such as marches, demonstrations and court cases to fight for civil rights.	Founded in 1914 by Marcus Garvey, by 1920 it had 2000 members and at its peak, membership stood at 250,000. Garvey believed that black people should not try to be a part of white society but should celebrate their blackness. He wanted black people to return to Africa. He was watched by the FBI, who found an excuse to imprison him after he was found guilty of postal fraud in 1925. Upon release he was deported to Jamaica, after which time the UNIA fell apart.

The treatment of Native Americans

Revised

Until the passing of the Indian Citizenship Act of 1924, America's native people had been denied full US citizenship. They had been forced to live on reservations, often on poor quality land which didn't support enough of the wild animals that Native Americans depended on. They were encouraged to reject their own culture and integrate fully into white society. Their children were sent away to boarding schools where they were taught English, forced to wear western clothes and encouraged to convert to Christianity. While the granting of citizenship gave them the right to vote, Native Americans, like black Americans, continued to be treated as second-class citizens and remained victims of racial intolerance.

Revision tasks

1. Use four to six key words to explain how black Americans and racial minorities were treated in the USA during the period 1910–29.
2. Construct your own spider diagram to show how some black Americans attempted to resist the policy of segregation.
3. 'Native Americans made no progress during the 1920s.' How far do you agree with this statement? First list the arguments for the statement – that they *did not* make progress during the 1920s. Then list the arguments against – that they *did* make progress during the 1920s.

The growth in popularity of the Ku Klux Klan during the early 1920s

Revised

Key facts

- Founded during the Civil War in 1866, the Ku Klux Klan (KKK) was a racist organisation which aimed to terrorise black Americans in the southern states who had just been freed from slavery.
- After a period of decline the movement was revived in 1915 by William J. Simmons following the release of the film *Birth of a Nation*.
- Membership of the Klan was only open to WASPS; members saw themselves as being superior to other races; they were anti-black, anti-Jew, anti-Catholic, anti-Communist and were against all foreigners.
- Concerns over immigration together with the Red Scare caused Klan membership to rise sharply in the early 1920s; 100,000 members in 1920 rising to 5 million members by 1925.
- The head of the Klan was the Imperial Wizard – a post held in the 1920s by Hiram Wesley Evans; Grand Dragons were in charge of each state.
- Klan members dressed in white robes and white hoods – the colour symbolising white supremacy; members carried the American flag and burnt crosses during their night-time meetings.
- Klan members carried out lynchings, floggings, brandings, mutilation, tar and feathering, kidnapping; they terrorised and inspired fear in non-WASPS.
- Klan members who carried out such deeds were rarely brought to justice; they knew their 'friends' in the courts would not convict them; many politicians resisted speaking out for fear of losing white votes; the federal government found it difficult to change long-held views of white supremacy in the south.

The decline of Klan membership in the late 1920s

Revised

The Klan suffered a sharp decline in membership following the conviction in 1925 of David Stephenson, the Grand Dragon of the Indiana Klan, for the rape and mutilation of a woman on a Chicago train. During the trial Stephenson spoke about illegal Klan activities which discredited the movement and brought it much bad publicity.

Revision task

Put together a timeline to show key developments in the history of the KKK and its activities between 1866 and 1929. You should include reference to membership and leadership above the line and examples of activities below.

Exam practice

Source A: Hiram Wesley Evans, Imperial Wizard of the Ku Klux Klan, speaking during an interview in 1924

'There are three great racial ideas which must be used to build a great America: loyalty to the white race, to the traditions of America and to the spirit of Protestantism. The pioneer stock must be kept pure. The white race must be supreme not only in America but in the whole world. The Klan believes the negroes are a special problem. Protestants must be supreme. The Roman Catholic Church is un-American and usually anti-American.'

How far does Source A support the view that the Ku Klux Klan was a racist organisation? **[5 marks]**

Answers online

Examiner's tip

For the 'how far' questions you need to make full use of the information contained in the source, including making reference to the attribution. You should add some of your own knowledge to this topic to help *make a judgement* as to 'how far' it supports or does not support the view.

4.3 Was the 1920s a decade of organised crime and corruption?

The reasons for prohibition

Revised

In January 1920 the 18th Amendment made it illegal to sell alcohol and the Volstead Act set down penalties for breaking this law. This became known as prohibition.

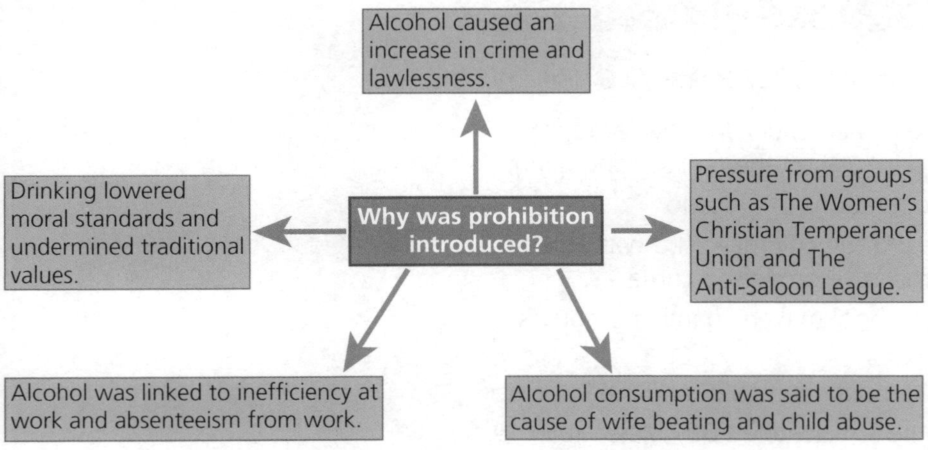

The difficulties in enforcing prohibition

Revised

Prohibition proved almost impossible to enforce and the law was openly ignored, particularly in the cities.

- The alcohol trade was driven underground and developed into organised crime under the control of powerful gangsters.
- **Bootleggers** such as Al Capone made large sums of money smuggling alcohol into the country.
- **Moonshiners** distilled their own illegal home brews.
- **Speakeasies** selling illegal alcohol sprang up in large numbers – by 1925 there were over 100,000 in New York.
- Government prohibition agents were too few in number to enforce the prohibition law and they were often open to bribery.

Key terms

Bootlegger – a person who supplies and distributes illegal alcohol

Moonshiner – a person who brews or distils their own illegal alcohol

Speakeasy – an illegal drinking shop

The end of prohibition

Revised

Prohibition proved impossible to enforce and by 1930 there was widespread opposition to it. There had been an increase in alcohol-related problems – by 1926, 50,000 people had died from drinking poisoned alcohol. It had led to the growth in organised crime and an increase in violence relating to gangster activities. After the Wall Street Crash many argued that making alcohol legal again would create jobs in the brewing and service industries, helping to reduce the high unemployment level. By introducing the 21st Amendment President Roosevelt ended prohibition in December 1933.

The growth in organised crime during the 1920s

Revised

The 1920s saw rapid growth in the number of criminal gangs. Prohibition provided them with the opportunities to engage in organised crime, providing illegal alcohol through bootlegging schemes. They controlled the speakeasies and diverted into other areas of crime – running protection rackets, gambling dens, prostitution houses and supplying drugs. Gangs increasingly fought each other for the control of this trade.

Al Capone and the St Valentine's Day Massacre

Revised

One of the most notorious gangsters of the 1920s was Al Capone.

- In 1921 Capone followed his gangster leader Johnny Torrio from New York to Chicago and quickly rose up the ranks in the gang.
- In 1925 he took over Torrio's operations in Chicago.
- By bribing senior police chiefs and the city mayor he was able to build up and operate a vast empire of organised crime.
- His empire included speakeasies, bookmakers, gambling houses, brothels, nightclubs and breweries.
- Capone had over 200 rivals killed between 1925 and 1929.
- The most serious incident was the St Valentine's Day Massacre in 1929. This was an attempt to kill the rival gangland leader Bugs Moran. The authorities could not find enough direct evidence to prosecute Capone.
- In 1931 Capone was found guilty of tax evasion and sent to prison. This really marked the end of the 'Age of the Gangsters'.

Corruption in government: President Harding and his 'Ohio Gang'

Revised

President Harding (1921–23) appointed many of his Ohio friends to posts in his cabinet and government offices. Harry Daugherty became Attorney-General and Albert Fall was appointed Secretary of the Interior. Some of these friends used their position to 'line their pockets'. The Head of the Veterans' Bureau was sent to jail for selling off veterans' hospital supplies for personal gain. But the biggest scandal concerned the Teapot Dome.

The Teapot Dome scandal

The leading figure in the scandal was the government minister Albert Fall (who was Secretary of the Interior):

- He leased out government land to drill for oil reserves at Teapot Dome, Wyoming, and in doing so he received illegal payments of over $400,000 from oil companies hoping to be granted the leases.
- Most of the money came from Harry Sinclair of the Mammoth Oil Company and Edward Doheny of the Pan-American Petroleum and Transport Company.
- Details of the secret deals were leaked to the press in 1922 and a government enquiry was demanded.
- The enquiry was not completed until 1927 when Fall was found guilty of bribery, fined $100,000 and sent to prison. Sinclair was also sent to prison but Doheny was acquitted. The leases were cancelled.

Exam practice

Describe the career of Al Capone. **[4 marks]**

Answers online

Examiner's tip

When answering 'describe' questions you need to ensure that you include at least 2–3 key factors. To obtain maximum marks you need to support them with *specific factual detail*, in this instance describing Capone's empire of crime, specific events like the St Valentine's Day Massacre and his eventual arrest, trial and imprisonment.

Revision tasks

1. 'Gangsters were solely responsible for the increase in organised crime in America during the 1920s.' How far do you agree with this statement? Copy and complete the table below.

Arguments in favour	Arguments against

2. Use four to six key words to show how the Teapot Dome scandal is an example of corruption in government.

Chapter 5 The rise and fall of the American economy, 1910–1929

Key issues

You will need to demonstrate good knowledge and understanding of the key issues of this period. These are:

- What were the causes of the economic boom?
- How did this prosperity affect American society?
- Why did the boom period come to a sudden and dramatic end in 1929?

5.1 What were the causes of the economic boom?

The US economy between 1910 and 1929

Revised

The US economy experienced growth following the outbreak of war in Europe in 1914 but in the years immediately after the war, 1919–22, there was a slowdown in economic activity. This was due to:

- the return of demobbed US soldiers from Europe which led to a rise in unemployment
- Europe beginning to recover and becoming less reliant upon America for food and manufactured goods
- a large number of strikes across America, especially in the textile, coal and steel industries, which occurred in this period.

By 1921 over 5 million men were registered as unemployed. However, by 1922 the economy was showing signs of recovery and it quickly entered a boom period which lasted until the autumn of 1929. The causes of this boom were due to a number of long-term factors and more immediate factors. An examination of one factor on its own does not explain why this growth took place, in reality it was caused by a number of factors which were inter-related.

Key term

Economic boom – a period of time when individual incomes and company profits increase

Revision task

Make a copy of the table below. Using the information from the diagrams on page 45, explain how each of the following factors helped the US economy to grow during the 1920s.

Key factor	How it helped the economy to grow
Availability of resources and labour	
Development of new technology	
Investors buying shares	

Long-term factors for the economic boom

Natural resources
- America had plentiful supplies of raw materials such as oil, coal, wood and iron ore

Cheap labour force
- immigration from Europe provided plentiful supply of cheap, unskilled labour

Protection of home industries
- policies and attitudes of the Republican presidents
- introduction of tariffs

Confidence in the US economy
- people had the confidence to invest
- they were prepared to buy goods, invest in companies and take out loans

Impact of the First World War
- America kept out of the war until 1917 and this had advantages
- she was able to supply Europe with food, raw materials, munitions
- US banks loaned money to Europe and US businessmen invested in Europe
- war stimulated technological advances such as mechanisation and the production of new materials like Bakelite (plastic)

Spread of electricity
- by 1929 most US cities had electricity
- electrification enabled the development and spread of a range of household domestic goods

More immediate factors for the economic boom

Technological change
- spread of electricity provided a cheap, flexible, more reliable source of power
- new manufacturing techniques using the conveyor belt, assembly line and mass-production
- availability of new materials such as Bakelite
- new building materials such as steel girders for skyscrapers

Speculation
- people became over-confident buying shares, believing that prices would continue to rise
- many bought on the margin

Too easy availability of credit
- banks were more willing to offer loans
- increasing use made of hire purchase (HP)

Growth in consumerism
- wages increased by 8% between 1923 and 1929 giving people more buying power
- greater range of household gadgets for sale
- availability of cheap credit
- spread of electricity
- effective use of advertising

Growth of stock market
- value of stocks and shares rose steadily between 1923 and 1929
- sharp rise in share prices 1928–29
- more and more people began to speculate when buying shares

How did the attitudes and policies of the Republican presidents contribute to the economic boom?

Key term

Speculation – buying shares on the stock market, often with borrowed money, hoping for a quick profit

Republican presidents of the 1920s

Revised

During the 1920s America was governed by an unbroken chain of three Republican presidents. This allowed for consistency of policy, the driving force of which was the idea of limited interference by government in the running of the economy.

Key term

Laissez-faire – policy of non-interference in the running of the economy

President	Warren Harding	Calvin Coolidge	Herbert Hoover
Years as president	1921–23	1923–29	1929–33
Key economic policies	'Back to normalcy'	**Laissez-faire**	Rugged individualism

Key policies adopted by the Republican presidents

Revised

- **'Back to normalcy'**
  - This was the policy of President Harding.
  - He wanted to reduce and limit government interference in the economy which had grown substantially during the war years.
  - He also wanted to reduce the tax burden on the rich.
- **Laissez-faire**
  - President Coolidge believed that the government should have only limited involvement in the day-to-day running of the economy.
  - By reducing regulations businessmen would be free to make their own decisions.
- **Rugged individualism**
  - This was the belief that people achieved success through their own hard work.
  - People should not expect the government to do things for them, they should fend for themselves.
- **Protectionism**
  - **Tariffs** were imposed on imported goods to limit competition from foreign imports.
  - Tariffs made European goods more expensive and encouraged the sale of American products.
  - The Fordney–McCumber Tariff Act (1922) raised import duties to their highest ever levels.

Key term

Tariff – a tax on foreign goods coming into a country

Exam practice

Describe how the policies of the Republican presidents aimed to help the US economy to grow during the 1920s. **[4 marks]**

Answers online

Examiner's tip

When answering 'describe' questions you need to ensure that you include at least 2–3 key factors. To obtain maximum marks you need to support them with specific factual detail, in this instance describing the policies of laissez-faire and protectionism, and the presidents' belief in rugged individualism.

5.2 How did this prosperity affect American society?

Key features of the new consumer society

Revised

- **Advertising**
  - More and more firms invested in advertising campaigns to increase sales and profits.
  - People had greater access to the media through newspapers, magazines, the radio and the cinema.
  - Development of sophisticated advertising techniques such as catchphrases, colourful adverts, targeting audiences, e.g. women for household appliances.
  - Growing popularity of catalogues led to growth in 'mail order' sales.
  - The availability of credit meant that people could 'buy now, pay later' using hire purchase.

- **Household appliances and electrical goods**
  - By 1927 two-thirds of US homes had electricity which stimulated demand for electrical goods.
  - The market was flooded with a new range of household electrical appliances such as vacuum cleaners, washing machines, refrigerators, irons, radios and gramophones.
- **New types of consumer stores**
  - Development of department stores which sold a range of **consumer goods**.
  - The first supermarket (the Piggly Wiggly store) opened in 1916 in Memphis, Tennessee.
  - Chain stores began to appear (F.W. Woolworth & J.C. Penney).

Key term

Consumer goods – manufactured goods available to buy by the majority of ordinary people, such as watches, vacuum cleaners, radios

The influence of the car industry in the economic boom

Revised

The car industry played a very important role in the boom of the 1920s, leading the way in technological developments and stimulating growth in other industries.

- Henry Ford led the way in introducing new methods of production. By 1913 Ford had pioneered the use of the electric conveyor belt and **assembly line**. The conveyor belt carried the partly assembled car past gangs of men spaced along the line, each gang performing a specific task. The parts they needed were supplied to them through overhead conveyor belts.
- The time to assemble Ford's Model T was reduced from 13 hours to 1 hour 33 minutes.
- **Mass production** methods caused the cost of the Model T to fall (1914 – $850; 1926 – $295).
- To offset the boredom of repetitive work, Ford doubled wages to $5 a day by 1914.
- His factory in Detroit operated 24 hours a day, using a 3 x 8 hours shift system and employing 80,000 people.
- The Model T, nicknamed 'Tin Lizzie', was the world's first mass-produced car using standardised parts and one colour – black.
- Ford used modern advertising techniques to sell his cars, and also introduced hire purchase.
- By 1925 half the world's cars were Model T's.
- Other firms copied Ford's use of mass production – Chrysler and General Motors.

Key terms

Assembly line – a line of workers and machines in a factory assembling a product

Mass production – manufacture of goods on a large scale using a standardised mechanical process

The impact of the car industry on the other sectors of the American economy

Revised

Mass production of cars stimulated growth in feeder industries such as steel, wood, rubber, leather and petrol. The increase in the number of cars stimulated road construction, which in turn led to the building of gas stations, motels and restaurants. It encouraged the development of suburbs. It transformed buying habits and hire purchase became the acceptable means of buying costly items. Car ownership benefited rural areas, making farmers less isolated and more mobile.

Other sectors of the economy that experienced a boom

Revised

- **Transport system**
  - More cars demanded more roads; miles of surfaced roads had doubled by 1929.
  - There was an increase in commercial transport; the number of vans on the road had doubled to 3.5 million by 1929.
  - This was the time of the birth and growth of civil aviation; in 1929 there were 162,000 flights.
- **Construction industry**
  - Economic growth created a demand for new buildings such as factories and houses.
  - The development of new materials enabled construction of new types of buildings such as skyscrapers.
  - New York witnessed a boom in skyscrapers – e.g. Woolworth Building (1913), Empire State (1931).

Revision task

Explain how each of the following contributed to the growth of the US economy in the 1920s.

- New consumer society
- Car industry
- Transport and construction

The groups and sectors that did not prosper during the boom period

Revised

Not all Americans experienced the economic boom of the 1920s and over 60 per cent of the population lived close to or below the poverty line.

- **Farmers**
  - A decline in European markets after 1918 led to a fall in food prices.
  - Over-production due to increased mechanisation meant farmers increasingly struggled to find a market for their produce.
  - Many were forced to borrow money and struggled to keep up with their mortgage payments.
  - Those who lost their farms ended up as **hobos**.
  - Total farm income fell from $32 billion in 1919 to $13 billion in 1928.

Key terms

Hobo – an unemployed wanderer/drifter seeking a job

Sharecropper – a tenant farmer who gave a share of his crop as rent

- **Black Americans**
  - They experienced the hardship associated with segregation in the southern states.
  - Many were labourers or **sharecroppers** who worked long hours and lived in slum conditions.
  - Conditions were also hard for those who had migrated to the northern cities; they lived in ghettos and remained 'the last to be hired and first to be fired'.
  - 750,000 black farm workers lost their jobs during the 1920s.

- **Immigrants**
  - These people were viewed as a source of cheap labour.
  - They received low wages.
  - They experienced prejudice and discrimination.
  - The unemployment rate amongst new immigrants remained high throughout the 1920s.

- **Trade Unions**
  - A large number of strikes in the early 1920s and the Red Scare damaged union membership.
  - Employers like Henry Ford were anti-union and refused to employ union members.

- **Older traditional industries**
  - The coal industry faced increased competition from oil, gas and electricity; there was more foreign competition from cheap imports; many mines were forced to close; there was an increase in strikes and industrial unrest within the industry.
  - The railroad industry faced increasing competition from the development of a national road network; the growth in car ownership made business very difficult; companies found it harder to generate profits.
  - The shipbuilding industry entered a period of sharp decline following high production during the war years.
  - The textile industry faced increasing competition from new man-made fibres (e.g. rayon); the change in women's fashions, e.g. with shorter dresses, reduced the amount of cloth needed; there was competition from cheaper foreign imports; many textile mills were forced to close down.

Revision task

Use the information in this section to explain why each of the following groups/sectors did not prosper in the 1920s.

- Farmers
- Black Americans
- Immigrants
- Trade Unions
- Older traditional industries

Exam practice

Source A: A poor family of farm workers living in the mid-West in the 1920s

What does Source A tell you about the lifestyle of some farmers during the 1920s? **[2 marks]**

Answers online

Examiner's tip

In this type of question you need to look into the picture and pick out relevant details. You should also make use of what is said in the caption. Aim to write two sentences. In this instance the source shows how poor some farmers were, with families living in poverty and having rags for clothes.

5.3 Why did the boom period come to a sudden and dramatic end in 1929?

A combination of long-term and short-term factors caused an end to the boom period.

Long-term factors for the end of prosperity

Revised

- **Over production**
  - **Over production** in industry meant the market became saturated with unsold consumer goods; factories were forced to cut prices and wages, and eventually lay off workers.
  - Over production in agriculture due to increased mechanisation and lower sales to Europe caused a fall in prices, forcing many farmers out of business.

Key term

Over production – producing too many goods

- **Falling demand for consumer goods**
  - The uneven distribution of wealth meant that those who could afford the new consumer goods had already bought them; those who could not afford them (close to 60 per cent of the population) got no nearer to being able to buy them.
  - Manufacturers failed to read the market and cut production.
  - Tariffs hindered trade and many foreign governments copied the US and introduced tariffs, making it harder to sell American goods abroad.
- **Boom in land and property values**
  - House and land prices rose sharply during the early 1920s, especially in Florida which experienced a boom.
  - After 1926 there was a dramatic fall in property prices which left many homeowners with **negative equity**.
  - This was a warning that the economy was slowing down but it was largely ignored by investors.
- **Poorly regulated banking sector**
  - Banks operated under limited regulation.
  - Many small banks failed to keep sufficient financial capital in reserve to support them during an economic downturn.
  - The banks would be quick and easy casualties in the crash of October 1929 (see page 51).

Key term

Negative equity – people owned property worth less than what they had originally paid for it

Short-term factors for the end of prosperity

Revised

- **Over speculation on the stock market**
  - Share prices had risen to unrealistic levels.
  - Investing in stocks and shares had become a popular pastime.
  - The number of shareholders had risen from 4 million in 1920 to 20 million in 1929.
  - In 1925 the stock market value of shares stood at $27 billion; by October 1929 it had reached $87 billion.
  - The lack of regulation by the government encouraged more and more speculation.
- **Availability of easy credit**
  - The availability of easy credit meant that many bought 'on the margin'.
  - People borrowed money to buy shares, believing they would continue to rise in value, then they would sell them at a profit and repay the loan.
  - By 1929, 75 per cent of the purchase price of shares was borrowed: an enormous amount of borrowed money riding on the bet that prices would keep going up.

Revision task

Make a list of the long- and short-term causes of the end to the economic prosperity of the 1920s. Number your list in order of importance. Give reasons why you think your number one is the most important cause.

Exam practice

Source A: A comment made in 1928 by John J Raskob, Director of General Motors

'If a man buys $15 worth of shares a month, he will, at the end of 20 years, have at least $80,000 and an income from investments of $400 a month. I am firm in my belief that anyone can not only be rich, but ought to be rich.'

How far does Source A support the view that many Americans were encouraged to buy shares in the 1920s?

[5 marks]

Answers online

Examiner's tip

For the 'how far' questions you need to make full use of the information contained in the source, including making reference to the attribution. You should add some of your own knowledge to this topic to help *make a judgement* as to 'how far' it supports or does not support the view.

The Wall Street Crash

Revised

When several big investors started to sell large numbers of shares in the autumn of 1929, small investors panicked. There was a rush to sell, causing share prices to plummet.

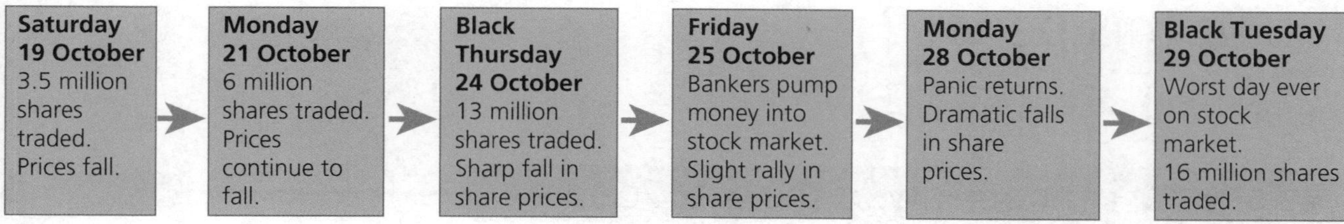

↑ **Key events in the Wall Street Crash**

The immediate effects of the Wall Street Crash

Revised

- The US stock market collapsed. Shares were worth only a fraction of what they had been.
- Many shareholders lost everything. There was an increase in suicides.
- There was a loss of confidence in the financial sector. Many banks went bust.
- People began to tighten their belts. There was less consumer spending.
- Unemployment rose sharply. Firms began to lay off workers.

America was entering the period of the Great Depression; the 'Roaring Twenties' had come to a dramatic end. A popular saying of the period was introduced: *'In Hoover we trusted, now we are busted.'*

Revision task

How did the Crash affect Americans? Find four to six key words for your answer.

Examiner's tip

When answering 'describe' questions you need to ensure that you include at least 2–3 key factors. To obtain maximum marks you need to support them with *specific factual detail*. In this instance describe the events on key days such as Black Thursday and Black Tuesday, noting the number of shares sold each day and how it all led to the sudden and dramatic collapse of the US stock market.

Exam practice

Describe the Wall Street Crash of October 1929. **[4 marks]**

Answers online

Chapter 6 Changes in American culture and society

Key issues

You will need to demonstrate good knowledge and understanding of the key issues of this period. These are:

- How did popular entertainment develop during this period?
- How did the lifestyle and status of women change during this period?
- Why did sport and other leisure activities witness so much growth during this period?

6.1 How did popular entertainment develop during this period?

The era of the silent movie

The growth in popularity of the silent cinema

Revised

After the First World War the silent cinema developed as the main form of entertainment and its growth was dramatic:

1910	8000 cinemas
1926	17,000 cinemas
1930	303,000 cinemas

Key term

Escapism – attempt to avoid reality by indulging in pleasurable fantasies

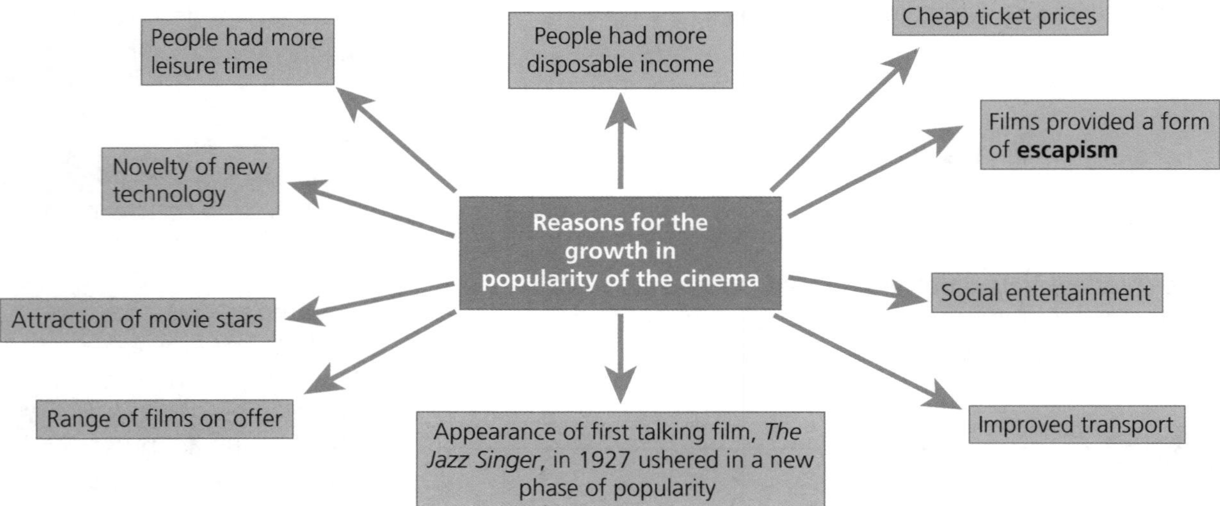

Hollywood – the centre of the film industry

Revised

Hollywood emerged as the centre of the film industry for these reasons:

- The attractive climate – there were few days of rain.
- The variety of landscape locations – desert, mountains, rivers, coast.
- Emerging production companies built studios there – Paramount, Warner Brothers, Columbia, Metro-Goldwyn-Mayer (MGM).
- The range of films produced – westerns, crime stories, romantic tales, slapstick comedy.
- Movie stars moved to live in the Los Angeles area.

Revision task

Explain how each feature helped to make the cinema grow in popularity during the 1920s:

- Leisure time
- Movie stars
- Novelty of new experience
- Escapism

The impact of movie stars

Revised

Through successful marketing and advertising campaigns, film studios helped build up the reputations of movie stars who developed cult followings:

Star	**Rudolph Valentino (1895–1926)**
Genre	Romantic star
Noted films	*The Four Horsemen of the Apocalypse* (1921) (first film to take 1 million dollars); *The Sheik* (1921)
Significant facts	First male star to be sold on sex appeal; 100,000 fans attended his funeral in 1926

Star	**Clara Bow (1905–65)**
Genre	Glamour star
Noted films	*It* (1927); *The Wild Party* (1929)
Significant facts	Referred to as the 'It Girl' because of her sex appeal; represented the **flapper** image

Star	**Charlie Chaplin (1889–1977)**
Genre	Slapstick comedy star
Noted films	*The Kid* (1921); *The Gold Rush* (1925)
Significant facts	His trademark was a tramp-like image: he wore an ill-fitting suit, bowler hat and cane; he made a successful transition from silent movies to talkies

Key term

Flapper – a fashionable young woman of the 1920s who wore short skirts, listened to jazz and challenged acceptable behaviour

Criticism of the movie industry

Revised

The film industry did receive some criticism. Movies were accused of lowering moral standards and of using movie stars as sex symbols. The lifestyle of some Hollywood stars attracted criticism, especially concerning stories of wild parties and love affairs. In an attempt to improve its image the film industry introduced its own 'Hays Code of Practice' and in 1928 set up the Oscars to celebrate what was best in the movies.

Exam practice

Explain why some Americans were critical of the movie industry. **[5 marks]**

Answers online

Examiner's tip

In 'explain why' questions you need to give two or more reasons, supporting your answer with specific factual detail. In this instance you need to talk about how groups like religious fundamentalists were critical of the lifestyle of the movie stars and the portrayal of such stars as sex symbols. You could also mention the lowering of moral standards.

The development of popular music and culture

The development of jazz music

Revised

Jazz developed in the southern states of America from traditional forms of black music such as ragtime and the blues. Many black musicians could not read music so they improvised, playing to their own beat and rhythm, making up the tune as they went along. **Jazz** became increasingly popular during the 1920s in the new nightclubs and speakeasies. Jazz was associated with the new flapper lifestyle and the new fashionable dances such as the Charleston.

Key term

Jazz – improvised, rhythmic music developed by black Americans in the 1920s

Leading jazz artists

Bessie Smith (1894–1937)	Duke Ellington (1899–1974)	Louis Armstrong (1901–71)
Vocalist	Pianist	Trumpeter
Greatest blues singer of the 1920s. Known as the 'Empress of the Blues'	Celebrated pianist. Leader of a ten-piece jazz band in New York	Displayed a unique talent on both the trumpet and cornet. From New Orleans he moved to Chicago, the jazz capital, and played in the Creole Jazz Band

The impact of the radio

Revised

By the end of the 1920s over 50 million Americans listened to the radio. Over 40 million US homes had a radio and listening to the radio became one of the most popular forms of entertainment during this period. Why?

- The spread of electricity.
- Mass production made radio sets available at reasonable prices – the accessibility of higher purchase meant people could borrow money to buy them.
- The radio enabled people to keep up to date with news and current affairs.
- People could listen to live events, especially sporting fixtures like baseball and boxing matches.
- People could listen to the new jazz music.
- The radio encouraged families to socialise, allowing them to gather together to sit and listen to the radio.
- By 1930 there were over 600 radio stations across America, the largest being the National Broadcasting Company (NBC) established in 1926 and the Columbia Broadcasting System (CBS) established in 1927.
- The gramophone industry had been very healthy in 1910 and record sales peaked in 1921. However the spread of the radio, being a cheaper option, helped to cause a sharp reduction in sales.

The impact of the dancing and speakeasy culture

Revised

The slow formal dances of the pre-First World War period were replaced by the fast beat jives and rhythmic dances associated with jazz music. The new popular dances included the Charleston, the Black Bottom, the Vampire, the Shimmy and the Bunny Hug. Dance halls became popular and some, like the Cotton Club in New York, had live jazz bands performing.

Such lifestyles shocked the older generation and religious groups who blamed jazz music for causing a decline in moral standards. They considered these new dances to be too sexual and the nightlife behaviour to be scandalous.

Revision task

Use your knowledge to explain how each of the following contributed to the development of jazz culture in America:

- Jazz artists
- The radio
- Dancing and speakeasies

6.2 How did the lifestyle and status of women change during this period?

Attitudes to women before the First World War

Revised

- The lifestyle of women was restricted by social convention.
- Middle-class and upper-class women led secluded lives – single women had to be accompanied by a **chaperone**; it was considered unladylike to smoke and drink in public; women wore tight-waisted, ankle-length dresses; they wore little make-up.
- Working women occupied low-paid jobs – cleaning, dress-making, secretarial work.
- Women did not have the right to vote.

Key term

Chaperone – a married or elderly lady who accompanies a young girl where men are present

Attitudes to women after the First World War

Revised

America's entry into the war in 1917 afforded new opportunities for women. They could participate in the workplace and they helped facilitate a change of attitude.

- New labour-saving household gadgets released women from time-consuming chores.
- Advertising helped usher in new fashions and tastes, especially the new flapper lifestyle (see page 56).
- New job opportunities arose – by 1930, 2 million more women were employed than had been in 1920, but many of these jobs were low paid.
- The 19th Amendment granted women the right to vote; in 1924 Nellie Tayloe Ross of Wyoming became the first woman to be elected governor of a state.
- The influence of jazz culture encouraged the independent flapper lifestyle.

The flapper lifestyle

Revised

During the 1920s younger middle-class and upper-class women began to challenge traditional attitudes towards females. This resulted in the growth of feminism. The aim was to develop a more independent social life for women and adopt a more liberal lifestyle. Women who adopted this new approach were called flappers.

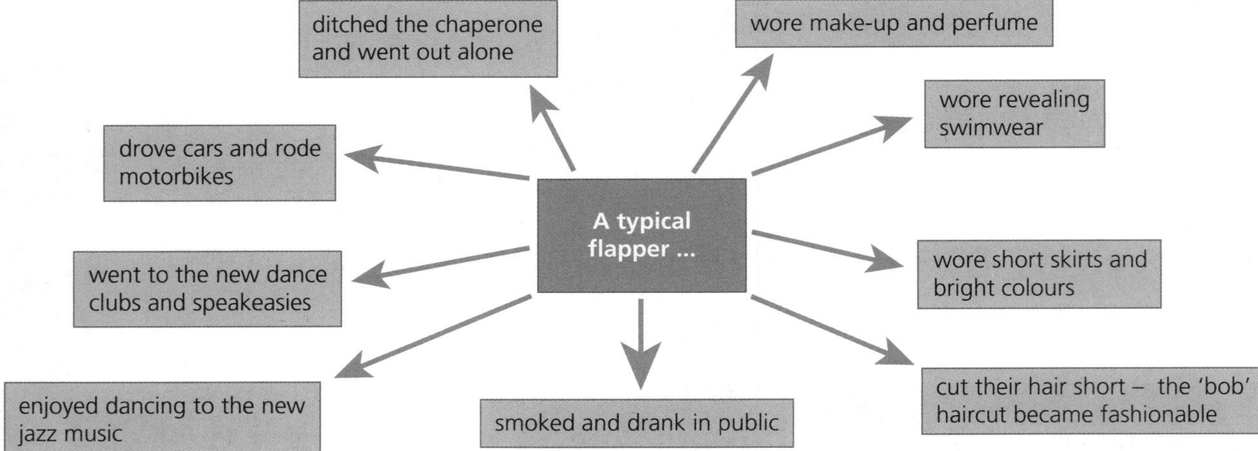

Flapper icons and role models	
Clara Bow	Called the 'It Girl' after playing a flapper in the 1927 film *It*. 'It' stood for sex appeal
Joan Crawford	She kissed, drank, smoked and danced the Charleston in films such as *Our Modern Maidens* (1929)

Opposition to the flapper lifestyle

Revised

- It was seen to be too extreme by many traditional groups, especially in the conservative rural areas.
- There was strong disapproval from religious groups who thought it was too sexual and too immoral.
- Some of the older generation formed the Anti-Flirt League in protest.
- Some flappers deliberately flouted the law and were arrested, bringing bad press to the feminist movement.
- The lifestyle was rejected by many poorer women who lacked the money and free time to follow the flapper lifestyle.

Exam practice

How important was the First World War in changing the lifestyle of women in America? **[5 marks]**

Answers online

Examiner's tip

In these 'how important/how successful' questions, you need to support your argument with factual detail and give a judgement. Here you need to compare the situation before 1917 with that after 1917, noting what had changed and what had stayed the same. This will enable you to give a judgement upon 'importance'.

6.3 Why did sport and other leisure activities witness so much growth during this period?

The growth in popularity of organised sport after the First World War

Revised

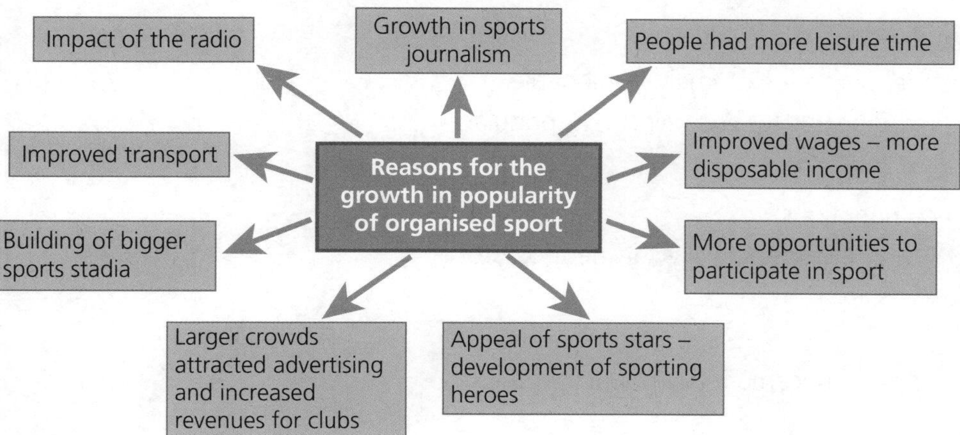

Revision task

Use the information in this section to help you explain how each of the following contributed to the growth in popularity of organised sport:

- Changes in people's disposable income and working hours
- The radio
- Advertising
- Baseball
- Boxing

Sporting heroes and their impact

Revised

Baseball	George Herman Ruth –'Babe Ruth' (1895–1948)	Played in major leagues from 1914 to 1935 Played for Boston Red Sox and New York Yankees First player to hit 60 home runs in one season
	Oscar Charleston (1896–1954)	Played in the Negro league Regarded as one of the greatest players Played for Indianapolis ABCs
Boxing	Jack Dempsey (1895–1983)	Held world heavyweight title from 1919 to 1926 Nicknamed the 'Manassa mauler': he won 66 of his 83 fights
	Gene Tunney (1897–1978)	Held world heavyweight title from 1926 to 1928 Defeated Jack Dempsey to win the title in 1926 Won 80 of his 86 fights
American football	Red Grange (1903–91)	Was the top player for the University of Illinois, the Chicago Bears and the New York Yankees In 2008 he was named the best college football player of all time
Tennis	Bill Tilden (1893–1953)	Ranked world number one throughout the 1920s By 1929 there were over 1000 tennis clubs across America
Golf	Bobby Jones (1902–71) and Walter Hagen (1892–1969)	The two most successful US golfers of the 1920s By 1927, 2 million Americans played golf regularly on 5000 courses

Fads and crazes

Revised

- **Dance marathons**
  - Growing popularity of non-stop dancing competitions, the last couple still standing claiming the prize money.
  - In 1923 Alma Cummings danced non-stop for 27 hours, wearing out six dancing partners.
- **New games and puzzles**
  - Mah Jongg, a Chinese game, became extremely fashionable.
  - Crosswords made their first appearance, becoming very popular.
- **Unusual crazes**
  - Live goldfish swallowing competitions.
  - Flagpole sitting: in 1923 Alvin 'Shipwreck' Kelly set the record of 49 days at Atlantic City.
- **Beauty contests**
  - Sponsored by newspapers, these became really popular in the 1920s.

The American heroes of the 1920s

Revised

- **Charles Lindbergh**
  - became the first to fly non-stop across the Atlantic (New York to Paris) on 20–21 May 1927
  - flew in a single-engined monoplane called the '*Spirit of St. Louis*'
  - the flight time was 33 hours, 39 minutes
  - became a national hero and received a tickertape parade in New York.
- **Amelia Earhart**
  - accompanied two male pilots and became the first female to fly across the Atlantic in 1929 (from Trepassey House, Newfoundland to Llanelli, Wales)
  - the flight time was 20 hours, 40 minutes.
- **Gertrude Ederle**
  - in 1926 she became the first woman to swim the English Channel
  - her swimming time was 14 hours, 30 minutes.

The impact of the motor car on leisure time

Revised

Mass-produced motor cars afforded millions of Americans the freedom to enjoy new leisure activities such as visits to the cinema, the sports stadia or the dancehall. It allowed families to explore the countryside and go on holidays and short breaks. The motor car served to create a more mobile society.

Revision task

'During the 1920s America was overtaken by a passion for fads, crazes and heroes.' Using information from this section, identify between four and six examples to support this statement, giving reasons for each choice.

Exam practice

The Roaring Twenties saw great change in the cultural and social life of many Americans. Was the growth of the cinema the most important development in American culture and society during this period? **[10 marks + 3 marks for spelling, punctuation and grammar (SPaG)]**

In your answer you should:

- discuss the importance of the growth of the cinema
- discuss other important developments in American culture and society.

Answers online

Examiner's tip

In the extended writing question you need to develop a two-sided answer which has balance and good factual support. In this instance you need to comment upon how the cinema developed into an important feature of American society. You then need to discuss other important developments such as the growth in the popularity of sport, the development of jazz music, dances and flappers. Remember to end with a clear judgement.

Section 3 Germany in transition, c.1929–1947

Chapter 7 The rise of the Nazi Party and its consolidation of power, c.1929–1934

Key issues

You will need to demonstrate good knowledge and understanding of the key issues of this period. These are:

- What was the impact of the Weimar period on the rise of the Nazis?
- How and why did Hitler get appointed Chancellor in January 1933?
- How did the Nazis consolidate their power during 1933–1934?

7.1 What was the impact of the Weimar period on the rise of the Nazis?

The political and economic problems of Weimar

The Weimar Republic

Revised

By the autumn of 1918 the German army was on the point of collapse. On 9 November the Kaiser abdicated and fled to the Netherlands. Germany became a **republic** and on 11 November the provisional government agreed to an armistice which brought Germany's fighting in the First World War to an end. Not all Germans welcomed the new republic and Berlin faced armed unrest from both left-wing and right-wing extremist groups. For this reason the newly elected Constituent Assembly, which met for the first time in January 1919, did so in the town of Weimar in southern Germany. This town gave its name to the **Weimar Republic**.

The Weimar Republic lasted from 1919 to 1933. During that time it was ruled by two Presidents – Friedrich Ebert (1918–25) and Paul von Hindenburg (1925–34). They often battled to keep weak and unstable governments in office. The Republic faced many weaknesses.

Key terms

Republic – a government in which supreme power is exercised by representatives elected by the people

Weimar Republic – following the abdication of the Kaiser in November 1918, Germany became a republic. It is named after the town of Weimar where the temporary government met to write a new constitution

The weaknesses of the Weimar Constitution

Revised

Weaknesses of the Weimar Republic

Appointment of Chancellor – the Chancellor was appointed by the President and was meant to be the leader of the largest party. After 1930 President Hindenburg appointed chancellors who did not lead the largest party and allowed them to rule using Article 48.

System of voting – use of **proportional representation** (PR) to elect members of the **Reichstag**.

Frequent changes of government – during the Republic there were nine elections, two each in the years 1923 and 1932. This resulted in weak and often unstable government.

Coalition government – the use of PR meant that parties obtained seats in the Reichstag in direct proportion to the total number of votes cast for them. This made it difficult for any one party to achieve an overall majority and resulted in coalition government.

Power of the President – during times of crisis the President could use Article 48 of the constitution to declare a 'state of emergency' and rule by Presidential decree. This was dangerous as it meant that laws could be passed without the approval of the Reichstag.

Until the appointment of Hitler most Chancellors came from moderate parties, yet they ruled over Reichstags which included extreme parties such as the Communists and Nazis, both of whom wanted to destroy the Republic.

Revision task

Copy and complete the following table to show how each factor helped to weaken the Weimar Republic.

	How this factor helped to weaken the Weimar Republic
Proportional representation	
Coalition government	
Article 48	

Key terms

Proportional representation – system where the number of votes won in an election directly determines the number of seats in parliament

Reichstag – the German parliament

Coalition government – a government made up of two or more political parties

The Treaty of Versailles, 1919

Revised

The new German government had no choice but to sign the Treaty of Versailles on 28 June 1919 which formally punished Germany for its involvement in the First World War. The majority of Germans were horrified by the terms and viewed the treaty as a great humiliation.

The treaty contained 440 clauses. The main terms were:

- **territorial terms:** Germany lost 13 per cent of its **land**, 6 million citizens and all her colonial possessions; Germany was forbidden to unite with Austria; Alsace-Lorraine was given to France; East Prussia was to be cut off from the rest of Germany by the Polish corridor; the Saarland was to be administered by the League of Nations
- **military terms:** the German **army** was limited to 100,000 men; it was forbidden to possess any tanks, heavy guns, aircraft or submarines; its navy was limited to ships of less than 10,000 tons; the Rhineland was to be demilitarised
- **financial terms:** under Clause 231 (War Guilt) Germany had to accept full responsibility for having caused the war and agree to pay **money** as reparations for the damage caused (a figure of £6600 million was fixed in 1921)
- **political terms:** Germany was forbidden to join the newly created League of Nations. Germany also had to accept **blame** for causing the war.

Key term

Reparations – war damages to be paid by Germany

Examiner's tip

For your exam you need to remember the key terms in the treaty. To remember these, use the acronym

LAMB.

L = LAND

A = ARMY

M = MONEY

B = BLAME

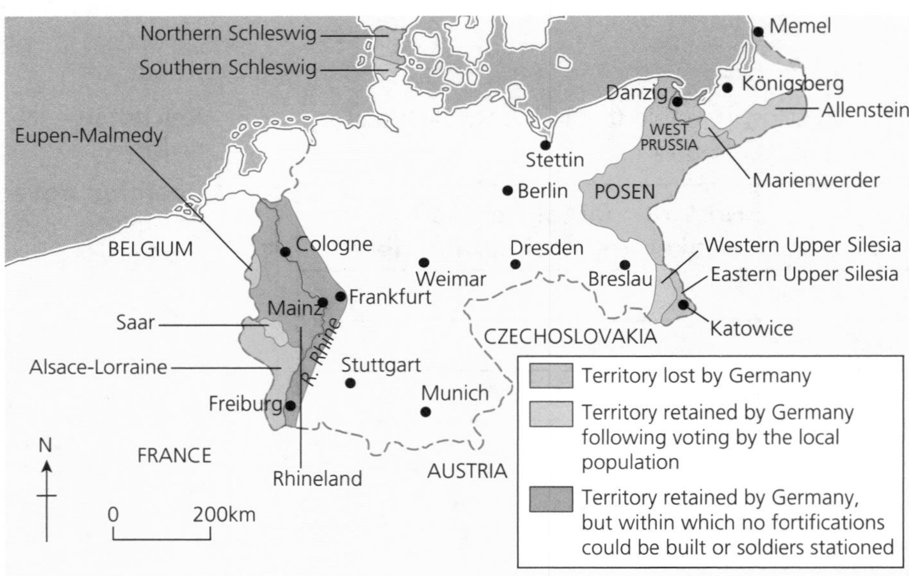

↑ **Territorial terms of the Treaty of Versailles**

The shame and humiliation of the Treaty, and the fact that the Germans were not allowed any role in negotiating the terms, gave ammunition to the opponents of Weimar, especially the extreme parties.

Exam practice

Source A: An extract from the German newspaper *Deutsche Zeitung*, June 1919

'Today in the Hall of Mirrors the disgraceful treaty is being signed. Do not forget it. The German people will with unceasing [constant] labour press forward to reconquer the place among nations to which is it entitled. Then will come vengeance [revenge] for the shame of 1919.'

Use the information in Source A and your own knowledge to explain why many German people disliked the Treaty of Versailles. **[4 marks]**

Answers online

Examiner's tip

This type of question requires you to do two things – discuss what is said in the source and add additional points from your own knowledge of this topic. In this instance the source talks about the shame and humiliation felt by many Germans and you could add to it by writing about the military, territorial or financial terms of the Treaty.

The early development of the Nazi Party

The origins of the Nazi Party

Revised

In 1919 Anton Drexler founded the German Workers Party (*Deutsche Arbeiter Partei,* DAP) in Munich, Bavaria. It was a right–wing, nationalistic party which stressed the ideal of a pure German people. While working for the army intelligence unit, Adolf Hitler attended a meeting in September 1919. He liked what he heard and was invited to join. His organisational ability was quickly recognised and in 1920 he was put in charge of the party's propaganda machine. In February 1920 Hitler and Drexler wrote the party's 'Twenty-Five Point Programme', which became its political manifesto. In July 1921 Hitler replaced Drexler as leader and he changed the name of the party to National Socialist German Workers Party (NSDAP). He adopted the title *Führer* (leader), developed a party symbol, the swastika, and introduced the raised arm salute.

Early growth of the Nazi Party

Revised

Party membership increased from 1100 members in June 1920 to 55,000 in November 1923. In 1921 Hitler set up the *Sturmabteilung* (SA) which was led by Ernst Rohm. Often referred to as the 'Brownshirts' because of the colour of their uniform or the 'Stormtroopers', this armed group of mostly ex-military men were charged with protecting Nazi speakers from attacks by rival political groups.

The political atmosphere in the early years of Weimar was one of chaos and disruption.

- In 1919 there was an attempted Communist revolution (the Spartacist Rising) in Berlin and in 1920 there was an attempted right-wing takeover (the Kapp **Putsch**).
- When Germany failed to make the second reparation payment in 1923, French and Belgium troops marched into the Ruhr to take control of the coalfields.
- In protest, German workers were encouraged to go on strike, the government supplying their wages. The government had to print more and more money and the result was the collapse of the currency and raging inflation.
- By November 1923 Germany was plagued by hyperinflation.

In this atmosphere of political and financial chaos, Hitler thought the time was right for the Nazi Party to seize power, first in the Bavarian state capital in Munich, followed by a march on Berlin.

Key term

Putsch – a political uprising

Revision task

Construct a timeline to show the key events in the history of the Nazi Party between January 1919 and November 1923.

The Munich Putsch, 8–9 November 1923

Revised

On the evening of 8 November 1923, Hitler and 600 SA men burst into a public meeting held in the Burgerbrau beer hall in Munich which was being addressed by Gustav von Kahr, the Bavarian Chief Minister. At gunpoint, von Kahr and the army chief von Lossow agreed to help in the planned takeover. They later informed the police and authorities of Hitler's plan.

When a Nazi force of 2000 SA men marched through Munich the following morning they were met by the police. In the clash, shots were fired in which sixteen Nazis and four policemen were killed. Hitler escaped the scene but was arrested two days later. Together with his main supporter, General Ludendorff, Hitler was put on trial and the Nazi Party was banned.

Hitler's trial started in February 1924 and lasted one month. It gave him national publicity. He criticised the '**November Criminals**', the Treaty of Versailles and the 'Jewish **Bolshevists**' who had betrayed Germany. While Ludendorff was let off, Hitler was found guilty of treason and sentenced to five years in Landsberg prison. He served only nine months.

Key terms

November Criminals – those politicians who had agreed to the signing of an armistice in November 1918

Bolshevists or **Bolsheviks** – followers of Lenin who carried out a Communist revolution in Russia in February 1917

The importance of the Munich Putsch

Revised

Whilst in prison Hitler had time to reflect. He realised that in order to win power the Nazi Party would have to change its strategy. Instead of an armed rising, the party would have to build upon recent publicity and work towards achieving a majority in the polls and be elected into office through the ballot box. He also used the time to complete his autobiography, *Mein Kampf* (*My Struggle*), which contained his political views.

Key term

Anti-Semitism – hatred and persecution of the Jews

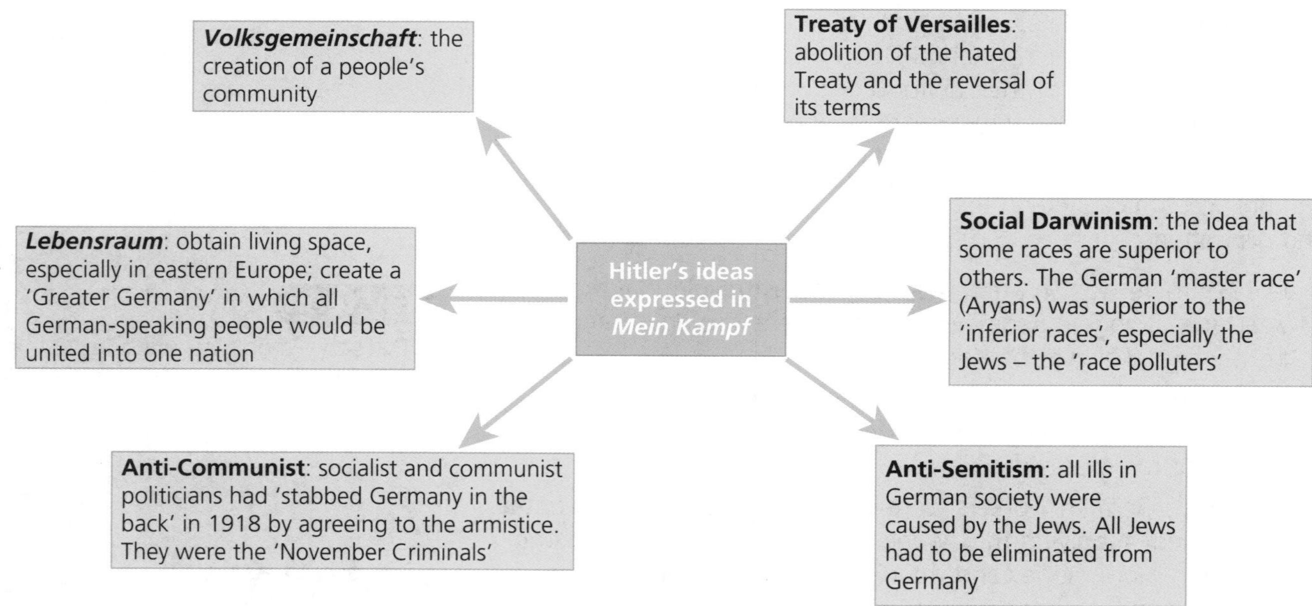

Revision task

Make a copy of the following table. Use the information in this section to complete each section, building up a picture of the importance of the Munich Putsch in the history of the Nazi Party.

	The importance of the Munich Putsch, November 1923
Aims of the Putsch	
Events of 8 November	
Events of 9 November	
The trial and sentence of the leaders of the Putsch	
Consequences of the Putsch for the Nazi Party	

Development of the Nazi Party, 1924–29

Revised

Upon his release from prison Hitler managed to have the ban on the Nazi Party lifted and he quickly set about reorganising and re-establishing his leadership:

- He created his own bodyguard, the **Schutzstaffel** (SS).
- He introduced the **Hitler Jugend** (Hitler Youth) to attract younger members.
- He used every opportunity to attack the weaknesses of Weimar and the Nazi Party began to attract support from all classes.
- In 1925 the Party had 27,000 members and by 1928 this had increased to over 100,000.

Despite these changes, the Nazis won only twelve seats in the Reichstag in the 1928 general election, having held 32 in 1924. The lack of success was largely due to the economic recovery brought about between 1924 and 1929 by the Chancellor and later Foreign Minister, Gustav Stresemann, whose policies dissuaded people from voting for the extreme parties.

Key terms

Schutzstaffel – the SS which originally started as Hitler's private bodyguard but which grew into a powerful organisation with wide powers; they wore black uniforms

Hitler Jugend – the Hitler Youth organisation set up in 1925 to convert young Germans to Nazi ideas

Revision task

Identify three ways in which the Nazi Party developed into a more powerful political force between 1924 and 1929.

7.2 How and why did Hitler get appointed Chancellor in January 1933?

The impact of the Wall Street Crash and the Great Depression

Revised

Much of the economic recovery in Germany in the late 1920s was heavily reliant upon American loans. Following the Wall Street Crash in October 1929 US banks recalled their loans. Depression hit the German economy:

↑ **The impact of US banks recalling loans in Germany**

Weimar politicians appeared to be doing too little too late and in desperation people increasingly began to turn to the extremist parties for solutions. Support for the Communists and Nazis rose sharply in the general election of September 1930.

Exam practice

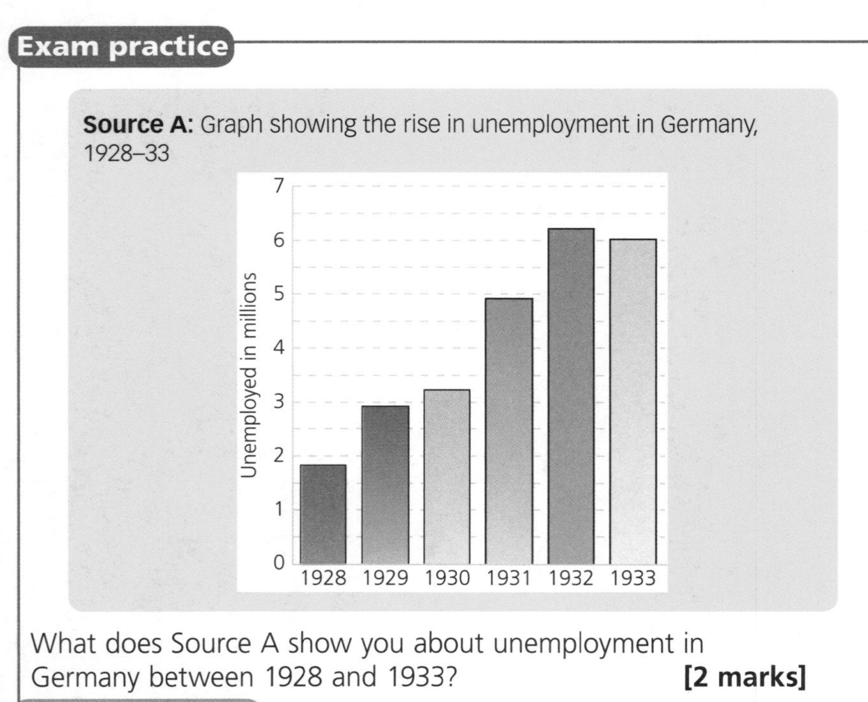

Source A: Graph showing the rise in unemployment in Germany, 1928–33

What does Source A show you about unemployment in Germany between 1928 and 1933? **[2 marks]**

Answers online

Examiner's tip

In this type of question you need to pick out specific detail from what you can see in the source and from the caption attached to it. In this context you need to say that the graph shows a sharp rise in unemployment, rising from under 2 million in 1928 to over 6 million in 1932. By 1933 it had begun to fall. It is important that you *'say what you see'*.

The end of parliamentary democracy: the coalition of Brüning

Revised

The harsh economic climate created severe problems for the weak coalition governments of Weimar and they soon collapsed, resulting in three general elections between 1930 and 1932. In March 1930 President Hindenburg appointed Heinrich Brüning of the Centre Party as Chancellor. Brüning lacked a majority and had to rely on President Hindenburg and Article 48 to allow him to rule using Presidential Decrees. From this point on, the Reichstag was used less frequently and the use of Article 48 marked the end of parliamentary democracy in Germany.

As the Depression deepened, Brüning's government became more and more unpopular. It was forced to cut unemployment benefits and Brüning became known as the 'hunger chancellor'. In May 1932 he resigned and in the general election which followed in July the Nazis polled their highest ever vote, securing 230 seats (37%) making them the largest party in the Reichstag.

	Elections to the Reichstag						
Party	**May 1924**	**Dec 1924**	**May 1928**	**Sept 1930**	**July 1932**	**Nov 1932**	**March 1933**
Social Democrats	100	131	152	143	133	121	120
Centre Party	65	69	61	68	75	70	73
People's Party	44	51	45	30	7	11	2
Democrats	28	32	25	14	4	2	5
Communists	62	45	54	77	89	100	81
Nationalists	106	103	79	41	40	51	53
Nazis	32	14	12	107	230	196	288

The coalitions of von Papen and von Schleicher

Revised

In March 1932 Hitler stood against Hindenburg in the Presidential elections. He polled 13.4 million votes against 19.3 million cast for Hindenburg. Hitler was becoming a well-known figure in German politics and following the Nazi Party success in the July election he should have been appointed Chancellor. Hindenburg, however, despised him and instead appointed the Nationalist leader Franz von Papen as his Chancellor.

Unable to obtain a working majority, von Papen was forced to call another election in November when the Nazi vote fell and they obtained 196 seats, 34 less than July. As the Nazi Party was still the largest party in the Reichstag, Hitler again demanded the post of Chancellor and again he was denied it. This time Hindenburg turned to General von Schleicher, the Minister of Defence, and appointed him Chancellor. His attempts to form a working majority failed and in January 1933 von Papen managed to persuade Hindenburg to appoint a **Nazi-Nationalist government** with Hitler as Chancellor and von Papen as vice-Chancellor. Von Papen believed he could control Hitler as only three of the eleven cabinet seats would be held by Nazis.

Key term

Nazi-Nationalist government – coalition of NSDAP (Nazi Party) and DNVP (German National People's Party) after January 1933

On 30 January 1933 Adolf Hitler became Chancellor of Germany – he had attained power by legal and democratic means.

German chancellors and their governments, 1930–33	
Brüning	March 1930–May 1932
Von Papen	May 1932–December 1932
Von Schleicher	December 1932–January 1933
Hitler–Von Papen	January 1933–March 1933

Revision task

Construct a timeline showing political developments in Germany between March 1930 and March 1933. Mark on unemployment figures, the presidential election, chancellors and governments.

Reasons for the Nazi electoral success

Revised

By 1932 the Nazi Party was the largest party in the Reichstag and had attracted electoral support from all sections of German society. There were many reasons for this electoral success:

- **Impact of the Depression:** the onset of the Depression created the political and economic conditions that caused millions of Germans to switch their voting habits and vote for the extreme parties. The moderate parties which had formed the coalitions appeared unable to tackle the worsening economic conditions. What was needed was radical action and the Nazi Party seemed to offer this.
- **The appeal of Hitler:** Hitler was a gifted public speaker who captivated his audiences. He projected the image of being the messiah, the saviour who would solve the problems facing Germany. Using his private plane he toured the country delivering speeches to mass audiences, offering something to all sections of society. He kept his message simple, blaming scapegoats for Germany's problems, especially the Jews and communists.
- **Use of propaganda:** Dr Josef Goebbels was in charge of the party propaganda machine. Through staging mass rallies, huge poster campaigns, using the radio and cinema, he ensured that the Nazi message was hammered home.
- **Financial support:** the Nazi Party could not have financed its electoral campaigns without large-scale financial backing from big industrialists like Thyssen, Krupp and Bosch. These industrialists feared a communist takeover and were concerned at the growth of trade union power. Hitler promised to deal with both fears.
- **The use of the SA:** the SA played a vital role in protecting Nazi speakers during election meetings and also in disrupting the meetings of their political rivals, especially the Communists. These 'bully boy thugs' of the party engaged in street fights with the political opposition.

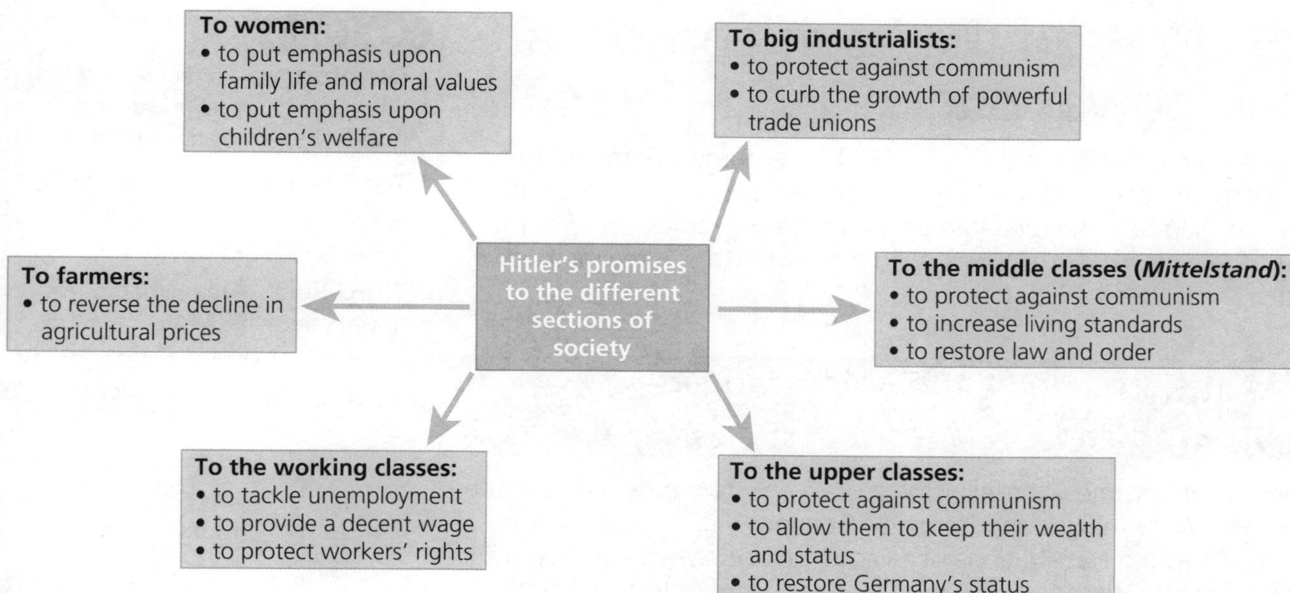

Revision task

Copy and complete the following table explaining how each of the factors listed helped the Nazis to win votes in the general elections of the early 1930s.

	How it helped the Nazis win votes in the elections
Impact of the Depression	
Use of propaganda	
Financial support	
Use of the SA	
Appeal of Hitler	

Exam practice

How important was Hitler in attracting support for the Nazi Party in the elections of 1930 and 1932? **[6 marks]**

Answers online

Examiner's tip

In the 'how important' questions you need to identify 2–3 key reasons why something was important, using specific factual detail to back up your comments. In this instance you should refer to the appeal of Hitler as a public speaker, his promises to help particular groups in society and his leadership and direction of the Nazi Party. Remember to provide a judgement on 'how important'.

7.3 How did the Nazis consolidate their power during 1933–1934?

Between January 1933 and August 1934 Hitler turned Germany into a one-party **dictatorship**. By August 1934 the posts of Chancellor and President had been merged into a new post – Führer (leader). For the next twelve years Germany was ruled by a **totalitarian** regime known as the **Third Reich**.

Key terms

Dictatorship – a regime in which the leader has total power and does not tolerate any opposition

Totalitarian – a state that has a one-party political system which holds total power

Third Reich – the period of Nazi government, 1933–45

The importance of the Reichstag Fire, 27 February 1933

Revised

When Hitler became Chancellor there were only two other Nazis in the Cabinet – Wilhelm Frick and Hermann Goering. Hitler's position was not strong as the Nazi-Nationalist alliance did not have a majority in the Reichstag. Hitler therefore persuaded Hindenburg to dissolve the Reichstag and call a general election for 5 March in which he hoped to increase the support for the Nazi Party. The Nazi propaganda machine helped deliver the party's message and the SA took to the streets to harass left-wing groups.

On 27 February, one week before the election, the Reichstag building was set on fire. A young Dutch Communist, Marinus van der Lubbe, was arrested and charged with starting the fire. Hitler used this event to his advantage:

- He argued that the Communists were planning a revolution.
- He persuaded Hindenburg to sign the 'Decree for the Protection of the People and State'.
- This gave Hitler the power to restrict free speech, limit the freedom of the press and imprison enemies of the state without trial.
- Communist and socialist newspapers were banned.

In the election on 5 March the Nazis won 288 seats but they still lacked an overall majority. A coalition was formed with the National Party. Hitler was disappointed as he needed two-thirds of the seats to be able to change the constitution, which was necessary to secure the passing of his Enabling bill.

The Enabling Act, 23 March 1933

Revised

On the day the Enabling bill was discussed in the Kroll Opera House (the temporary home of the Reichstag) Hitler banned the Communists from attending and encircled the building with SA men who prevented known opponents from entering. Absentees were counted as present and therefore in favour of the proposed bill. Promises were made by Hitler to the Catholic Centre Party to secure their votes. As a result the bill was passed, by 444 votes in favour to 94 against. Its passing marked the end of the Weimar Constitution. The Enabling Act became the 'foundation stone' of the Third Reich and it was used by Hitler to establish his dictatorship.

Use of the Enabling Act to establish the Nazi dictatorship

Revised

Through the use of the Enabling Act Hitler was able to establish his dictatorship and impose his policy of **gleichschaltung** (forcing into line):

Key term

Gleichschaltung – Nazi policy of forced coordination, bringing all social, economic and political activities under state control

Use of the Enabling Act

Control of the states: on 30 January 1934 the Law for the Restoration of the Reich abolished state assemblies and replaced them with Reich governors.

Purge of the civil service: on 7 April 1933 the Law for the Restoration of the Professional Civil Service removed Jews and political opponents of the Nazis from their posts in the civil service.

Control of the press: in October 1933 the Reich Press Law imposed strict control and censorship of the press.

Ban on political parties: on 14 July 1933 the Law against the Formation of Parties made the Nazi Party the only legal political party; Germany was now a one-party state; some parties had already disbanded voluntarily.

Trade Unions: on 2 May 1933 all trade unions were banned and replaced by the German Labour Front (Deutsche Arbeitsfront – DAF); strikes were made illegal.

The Night of the Long Knives, 30 June 1934

Revised

The SA had played a key part in the growth of the Nazi Party and as a reward their leader, Ernst Roehm, now wanted to incorporate the army into the SA. Roehm also wanted more government interference in the running of the country and he began pushing for a social revolution which would do away with Germany's class structure.

Hitler now saw the SA and its leadership as an increasing threat to his power. He needed the support of the army but the generals would never agree to Roehm's demands for the SA to control them. Hitler had to make a choice between the SA and the army. He decided upon the latter and on the night of 30 June 1934 he used the SS to carry out a purge. Codenamed 'Operation Hummingbird', and known as the Night of the Long Knives, over 400 'enemies of the state' were arrested and shot by the SS. They included Roehm, former Chancellor von Schleicher and Bavarian Chief Minister von Kahr.

The importance of the Night of the Long Knives

Revised

The Night of the Long Knives is seen as a turning point in establishing Hitler's dictatorship:

- It eradicated would-be opponents to Hitler's rule.
- It secured the support of the army.
- It relegated the SA to a minor role.
- It provided Himmler with the opportunity to expand the SS.

The death of Hindenburg: Hitler becomes Führer

Revised

On 2 August 1934 President Hindenburg died. Hitler seized the opportunity to combine the two posts of President and Chancellor and gave himself the new title of Führer (leader). He was now Head of State and Commander-in-Chief of the Armed Forces. That same day the officers and men of the German army were made to swear an oath of loyalty to the Führer. In a referendum on 19 August more than 90 per cent of votes agreed with his action. Hitler was now absolute dictator of Germany.

Revision tasks

1. Copy and complete the following table to show how each factor helped to increase Hitler's power and control over Germany.

	How this factor helped to increase Hitler's power and control over Germany
Reichstag Fire	
Decree for Protection of the People and State	
Enabling Act	
Night of the Long Knives	
Death of Hindenburg	

2. Which of these events were the most important in making Hitler dictator of Germany? Rank them in order of their importance, giving reasons for your choice.

Exam practice

Source A: A cartoon by David Low which appeared in the British newspaper, the *London Evening Standard* on 3 July 1934. Goering is standing to Hitler's right, dressed as a Viking hero, and Goebbels is on his knees behind Hitler.

How far does Source A support the view that Hitler increased his power following the Night of the Long Knives? **[5 marks]**

Answers online

Examiner's tip

In the 'how far' questions you need to give a judgement upon the accuracy of the information given in the source. In this instance you need to comment upon how the SA leaders are lying dead having been shot and the remaining SA men have both their arms up in submission to Hitler. The German army is on Hitler's side. The source supports the viewpoint but it is a British cartoon and is therefore likely to be biased in its interpretation.

Chapter 8 Changing life for the German people, 1933–1939

Key issues

You will need to demonstrate good knowledge and understanding of the key issues of this period. These are:

- How did Nazi economic and social policy affect life in Germany?
- How did Nazi political policy affect life in Germany?
- How did Nazi racial and religious policy affect life in Germany?

8.1 How did Nazi economic and social policy affect life in Germany?

Dealing with Germany's economic problems

Revised

When Hitler became Chancellor in January 1933 Germany had experienced more than three years of economic depression. Hitler immediately introduced a number of measures designed to reduce unemployment, which stood at 6 million.

- **Creation of the National Labour Service Corps (RAD):** from 1935 it was compulsory for all males aged 18–25 to serve in the RAD for six months, undertaking manual labour jobs. Workers lived in camps, wore uniforms and carried out military drill as well as work.
- **Public works programme:** men were put to work on public works schemes which included the building of 7000 km of autobahns (motorways), tree planting and the construction of hospitals, schools and houses.
- **Rearmament:** Hitler's decision to rearm transformed German industry and created jobs. Conscription was introduced in 1935 and the army was increased from 100,000 in 1933 to 1,400,000 in 1939. In 1933 3.5 billion marks was spent on producing tanks, aircraft and ships. By 1939 this figure had increased to 26 billion marks. Heavy industry expanded. Coal and chemical usage doubled between 1933 and 1939, while oil, iron and steel usage trebled.
- **Control of the economy:** in 1934 Hjalmar Schacht, President of the Reichsbank, was made Economic Minister. He believed in **deficit spending** to create jobs and used **Mefo bills** (credit notes) to finance public spending. In 1936 Schacht was replaced by Herman Goering as Economic Minister and he introduced the **Four-Year Plan** (1936–40). This was designed to speed up rearmament, prepare the country for war and establish the policy of **autarky** which was designed to make Germany self-sufficient, e.g. extracting oil from coal.

Key terms

Deficit spending – when the government spends more money than it receives in order to expand the economy

Mefo bills – credit notes issued by the Reichsbank and guaranteed by the government. They were used to fund rearmament

Four-Year Plan – a plan which aimed to make Germany ready for war within four years, giving priority to rearmament and autarky

Autarky – a Nazi government policy of making Germany self-sufficient with no foreign imports

- **Invisible unemployment:** unemployment fell dramatically, from 6 million in 1933 to 350,000 by 1939 (see graph on the right). However, these figures hid the true picture as they did not include Jews or women dismissed from their jobs, or opponents of the Nazi regime held in concentration camps.
- **Control of the workforce:** Hitler viewed trade unions as the breeding ground for socialism and communism. To avoid strikes and industrial unrest he banned the unions and in May 1933 replaced them with the German Labour Front (DAF). It had complete control over the discipline of workers, regulating pay and hours of work.
- **Rewarding the workforce:** to reward loyal workers the Strength through Joy (Kraft durch Freude – KdF) organisation was set up. It aimed to improve leisure time by sponsoring subsidised leisure activities and cultural events. These included concerts, theatre visits, sporting events, weekend trips, holidays and cruises. The Beauty of Work organisation aimed to improve working conditions through the building of canteens and sports facilities. In 1938 the Volkswagen (People's Car) Scheme was introduced, allowing workers to save five marks a week to buy their own car.

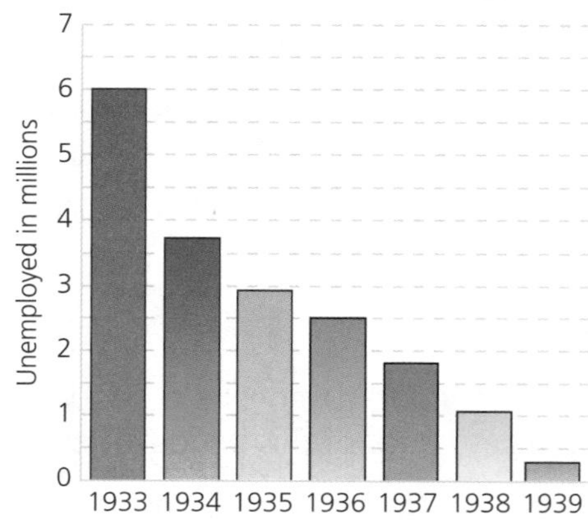

↑ **The fall in German unemployment, 1933–39**

Revision task

Identify five factors which drove forward Germany's economic recovery after 1933. Rank them in order of importance.

Nazi attitudes and policies towards women

Revised

- **Progress made by women during the Weimar period:** during the Weimar period women made substantial advances in German society. They had achieved equal voting rights with men; they had been encouraged to obtain a good education and had taken up careers in the professions, especially in the civil service, law, medicine and teaching. German women (who chose to) could go out unescorted, follow fashion, wear make-up, smoke and drink in public.
- **Nazi attitudes towards women:** Nazi attitudes were very traditional and they introduced policies which reversed many of the gains made by women during the 1920s. The Nazis viewed men as the decision makers and political activists, while women were relegated to being responsible for the home and for bringing up children. They discouraged women from wearing make-up, trousers, high heels and from dyeing their hair.
- **Nazi policies aimed at women:**

Key term

Aryan – Nazi term for a non-Jewish German; someone of supposedly 'pure' German stock

The Three K's	Law for the Encouragement of Marriage (1933)	Lebensborn (Life Springs) Programme (1936)
Instead of going to work women were encouraged to stick to the Three K's (*Kinder, Kuche, Kirche – Children, Kitchen, Church*). They were expected to give up their jobs, to get married and start a family.	This provided loans to encourage couples to marry, provided the wife left her job. Couples were allowed to keep one-quarter of the loan for each child born, up to four children. The Motherhood Cross medal was introduced to reward women with large families.	In an effort to boost the population, unmarried **Aryan** women were encouraged to 'denote a baby to the Führer' by becoming pregnant by 'racially pure' SS men.

Exam practice

Describe how life for women living in Germany changed between 1933 and 1939. **[4 marks]**

Answers online

Examiner's tip

In 'describe' questions you need to demonstrate specific knowledge, covering two to three key factors. In this instance you need to identify key areas of change in the lives of women, such as being forced to give up their jobs, adopting the lifestyle of the Three K's and being encouraged to have large families.

Nazi control of education

Revised

Hitler realised the importance of **indoctrinating** young people in Nazi beliefs. His aim was to turn them into loyal and enthusiastic supporters of the Third Reich. This was to be achieved through the control of education.

- Teachers had to belong to the Nazi Teachers' League; they had to promote Nazi ideas in the classroom and swear an oath of loyalty to Hitler.
- The curriculum was strictly controlled: 15 per cent of the timetable was devoted to physical education; for the boys the emphasis was upon preparation for the military; for the girls it was needlework and cookery to enable them to become good homemakers and mothers.
- Lessons started with pupils saluting and saying '*Heil* Hitler'. Every subject was taught through the Nazi point of view – biology lessons were used to study racial theory and the importance of the 'master race'; geography lessons were used to show how Germany was surrounded by hostile neighbours.
- Textbooks were rewritten to reflect Nazi views – history textbooks contained a heavy emphasis upon German military glory and the evils of Communism and the Jews who were blamed for the problems of the Depression.

Key term

Indoctrinating – making someone accept a system of thought without question

Nazi control of the German youth

Revised

The Nazis wanted to influence young people in school but also out of school. This was achieved through the Hitler Youth Movement which had existed since 1925. The Hitler Youth Law of 1936 made it difficult to avoid joining, blocking the promotion of parents who refused to allow their children to join. The Second Hitler Youth Law of 1939 made membership compulsory. By 1939 there were 7 million members. Baldur von Schirach was Reich Youth Leader.

There were several divisions of the Youth Movement, according to age:

Age	Boys	Girls
6–10	Pimpfen (Little Fellows)	
10–14	Jungvolk (Young Folk)	Jungmädel (Young Girls)
14–18	Hitler Jugend (Hitler Youth)	Bund Deutsche Mädchen (German Girls League)

- Boys were instructed in military skills such as shooting, map reading and drill; they took part in athletics, hiking and camping.
- Girls received physical training and learned domestic skills in preparation for motherhood and marriage; their groups had less emphasis upon military training.

Revision task

How did the Nazis attempt to control young people:

- in school
- during their free time?

8.2 How did Nazi political policy affect life in Germany?

By the end of 1934 Hitler controlled the Reichstag, the army and the legal system. It was now almost impossible for anyone to escape the power and grip of the Nazis.

The Nazi Police State

Revised

By 1934 Germany was a police state and the key organs for ensuring conformity were:

- **the SS (Schutzstaffel):** formed in 1925 as a bodyguard for Hitler they were part of the SA. They wore black uniforms and after 1929 they were led by Heinrich Himmler. After the Night of the Long Knives (see page 71), the SS replaced the SA as the main security force, responsible for the removal of all opposition to the Nazis within Germany. SS officers had to be pure Aryans. By 1934 the SS numbered 50,000.
- **the Gestapo (Secret State Police):** set up by Goering in 1933, in 1936 they came under the control of the SS and were led by Himmler's deputy, Reinhard Heydrich. The Gestapo became feared as they could arrest and imprison suspected 'enemies of the state' without trial. Many of those arrested ended up in concentration camps. By 1939, 160,000 people were under arrest for political crimes.
- **concentration camps:** the first concentration camp was opened in April 1933 at Dachau outside Munich and others soon followed at Buchenwald, Mauthausen and Sachsenhausen. Prisoners were classified into different categories and wore a coloured triangle to denote their crimes.

Control of the legal system

Revised

The Nazis aimed to control the courts and the legal system:

- Judges and lawyers had to belong to the National Socialist League for the Maintenance of Law and Order which forced them to accept Nazi policy. Those who refused were sacked.
- In October 1933 the German Lawyers Front was established and its 10,000 members swore an oath of loyalty to the Führer.
- In 1934 a new People's Court was set up to try enemies of the state. By 1939 it had sentenced over 500 people to death. The number of crimes punishable by death rose from 3 in 1933 to 46 in 1943. They included such crimes as listening to a foreign radio station.

Control of central and regional government

After 1933 Hitler reorganised central and regional government to ensure that all parts of it came under Nazi control:

- **Central government**: the Enabling Law (renewed every four years; see page 70) meant that the Reichstag was no longer needed to pass laws and it rarely met after 1933; Germany came to be governed by 'the will of the Führer' and Hitler made all the key decisions. Government policies were carried out by an elite core of Nazi leaders which included Hermann Goering, Josef Goebbels, Heinrich Himmler and, later, Martin Bormann. They competed to secure the attention of the Führer. The Civil Service was purged of non-Nazis and carried out policies without question.
- **Regional government:** in March 1933 Hitler closed down all state parliaments and divided the country into regions (Gau), each headed by a Reich Governor (Gauleiter). These men were loyal party officials directly appointed by the Führer and they had the power to appoint and dismiss the town mayor and all councillors and make state laws.

Through these means Hitler maintained a tight hold over what went on at the central, regional and local levels of government.

The use of propaganda and censorship

Revised

In March 1934 the Ministry for Popular Enlightenment and Propaganda was set up under Dr Josef Goebbels. The aim of the organisation was to control the thoughts, beliefs and opinions of the German people. It attempted to brainwash them through a variety of methods:

- **Cinema:** all films had to be given pro-Nazi story lines and film plots had to be shown to Goebbels before going into production; shown with all films were official newsreels which glorified Hitler and Nazi achievements.
- **Newspapers:** all newspapers were subject to strict censorship and editors were told what they could print; the German people only read what the Nazis wanted them to know.
- **Rallies:** an annual mass rally of over 100,000 was staged in September at Nuremberg to showcase the Nazi regime; floodlights, stirring music, flags, banners and marching columns followed by a speech by Hitler created an atmosphere of frenzy; spectacular parades were held on other special occasions.
- **Radio:** all radio stations were placed under Nazi control; cheap mass-produced radios were sold; radio sets were placed in cafés and factories and loudspeakers broadcast programmes in the streets.
- **Posters:** great use was made of posters to put across the Nazi message.
- **Books:** all books were censored and those published had to put across the Nazi message; over 2500 writers were banned; in May 1933 Goebbels organised the burning of banned books through mass bonfires.
- **The arts:** music, painting, sculpture, the theatre and architecture all had to portray the Nazi interpretation of German life and society, emphasising the qualities of the 'master race' and its heroic citizens.

Exam practice

Explain why the use of propaganda and censorship was so important to the Nazi regime. **[5 marks]**

Answers online

Examiner's tip

In 'explain why' questions you need to give two or more reasons, supporting your answer with specific factual detail. In this instance you need to talk about the importance of controlling what the German people heard and read, and of using these methods to brainwash them into accepting Nazi views.

Revision task

Use the information in this section to explain how each of the following factors helped the Nazis gain control over the German people:

- Use of the SS and Gestapo
- Control of the legal system
- Control over central government
- Control over regional and local government

8.3 How did Nazi racial and religious policy affect life in Germany?

Nazi racial policy

The master race and the subhumans

Revised

In *Mein Kampf* Hitler had spelled out his ideas on race. He argued that pure Germans – Aryans – formed the 'master race' and they were characterised by being tall, having fair hair and blue eyes. However, over time this race had been contaminated by 'subhumans' – the *Untermenshen*. In order to rebuild the 'master race' as a pure line, it would be necessary to introduce selective breeding, preventing anyone who did not conform to the Aryan type from having children and, in extreme cases, eliminating them. Measures were introduced to sterilise the mentally ill, the physically disabled, homosexuals, black people and gypsies. Among those groups who received widespread persecution were the Jews.

The Nazi policy of anti-Semitism

Revised

Anti-Semitism goes back to the Middle Ages and attacks upon Jews were common in Europe in the early twentieth century, particularly in Russia. The Nazis played upon existing hatred and found a scapegoat in the Jews, blaming them for Germany's defeat in the First World War, the hyperinflation of 1923 and the economic depression of 1929. Hitler had no master plan to eliminate Germany of its Jews and until 1939 most of the measures introduced against the Jews were uncoordinated.

To begin with, Jews were encouraged to leave the country – in 1933 there were 550,000 Jews living in Germany, by 1939 280,000 had emigrated (including Albert Einstein who left for America in 1933). Life for German Jews got harsher as the 1930s progressed, starting with acts of public humiliation, until the Nazis eventually took away their human rights.

Measures taken against German Jews, 1933–39	
April 1933	Boycott of Jewish shops and businesses
April 1933	Jews banned from working in the Civil Service and holding positions such as teachers, doctors, dentists, judges
October 1933	Jews banned from working as journalists
May 1935	Jews banned from entering the armed forces
September 1935	The Nuremberg Laws: the Reich Law on Citizenship took away from Jews the right of German citizenship; the Law for the Protection of German Blood and Honour made it illegal for them to marry or to have sexual relations with Aryans
November 1936	Jews banned from using the German greeting '*Heil* Hitler'
July 1938	Jews issued with identity cards; Jewish doctors, dentists and lawyers were forbidden to treat Aryans
August 1938	Jews forced to adopt the Jewish forenames of 'Israel' for a man and 'Sarah' for a woman

Measures taken against German Jews, 1933–39 (continued)	
October 1938	Jewish passports had to be stamped with the large red letter 'J'
November 1938	Kristallnacht (Night of Broken Glass): the murder of a Nazi official in Paris by a young Polish Jew resulted in the events of 9–10 November. In reprisal for the murder, Goebbels organised attacks on Jewish property in cities across Germany; so many windows were smashed that the event became known as the 'Night of Broken Glass'; over 7500 Jewish shops were destroyed, 400 synagogues burnt down and about 100 Jews were killed; over 30,000 Jews were arrested and taken to concentration camps; Jews were fined 1 billion Reichmarks as compensation for the damage caused
December 1938	Forced sale of Jewish businesses
February 1939	Jews forced to hand over precious metals and jewellery
April 1939	Jews evicted from their homes and forced into **ghettos**

Revision task

Give five examples of how life for Jews living in Germany became more difficult after 1933.

Key term

Ghetto – part of a city inhabited by a minority because of social and economic pressure

The Nazi treatment of the Church

Revised

Nazi attitudes towards religion

Hitler viewed the Church as a threat to Nazi policies but he also realised the importance of its support as Germany was a Christian country. Two-thirds of the population was Protestant and one-third was Catholic. Many Christians saw Nazism as a protection against the atheism of Communism and as an upholder of traditional family values and morals.

Nazi relations with the Catholic Church

In July 1933 Hitler signed a Concordat (agreement) with the Pope. This allowed the Catholic Church full religious freedom to operate without state interference and in return the Pope promised to keep the Church out of politics. Hitler soon broke this agreement – Catholic schools were taken out of Church control, Catholic youth groups were closed down and Catholic priests were harassed and arrested. In 1937 Pope Pius XI protested against the abuse of human rights. As a result 400 Catholic priests were arrested and sent to Dachau concentration camp.

Nazi relations with the Protestant Church

Many Protestants opposed Nazism and the **National Reich Church**. They were led by Pastor Martin Niemöller. In April 1934 he set up the Confessional Church which openly attacked the Nazi regime. In 1937 Niemöller was arrested and sent to a concentration camp. The Confessional Church was banned.

Key term

National Reich Church – a new Nazi Church set up to attract worshippers away from traditional places of worship

The creation of the National Reich Church

In 1933 the National Reich Church was set up to 'Nazify' the Protestant Church structure. It was led by Reich Bishop Ludwig Müller. The Bible, cross and other religious objects were removed from the altar and replaced with a copy of *Mein Kampf*, a portrait of the Führer and a sword. It seemed as if the Reich Church had been 'coordinated' through the process of gleichschaltung (see page 71). However, the Nazis never succeeded in destroying the Church in Germany. Priests and pastors had to make the choice of staying quiet and giving the appearance of conformity or being arrested by the Gestapo; most opted to support Hitler and conform.

Revision task

How far did the Nazis succeed in controlling the Church?

Exam practice

The Nazis introduced changes which affected the lives of ordinary Germans. Did life under Nazi rule benefit all people living in Germany between 1933 and 1939?

In your answer you should:

- discuss those Germans who did benefit from Nazi rule
- discuss those Germans who did not benefit from Nazi rule.

[10 marks + 3 marks for spelling, punctuation and grammar (SPaG)]

Answers online

Examiner's tip

In the extended writing question you need to develop a two-sided answer which has balance and good factual support. In this instance you need to comment upon those who benefitted from the sharp fall in unemployment, the creation of jobs and reward schemes for loyal workers (KdF). You then need to comment upon those who did not benefit, such as the Jews and gypsies for whom life grew more and more difficult. Remember to end with a clear judgement.

Chapter 9 War and its impact on life in Germany, 1939–1947

Key issues

You will need to demonstrate good knowledge and understanding of the key issues of this period. These are:

- How was life affected during the war years?
- How much opposition was there to the Nazis within Germany during the war years?
- What was the situation in Germany following total defeat in the war?

9.1 How was life affected during the war years?

A study of life on the **home front** can be divided into two phases. The first covered the years 1939–41 when the war was going well for Germany and there was only limited impact upon the civilian population. The second phase covered the period 1942–45 when a number of key military defeats led to increasing economic hardship and social misery, culminating in the invasion of Germany by Allied forces and ultimate defeat.

Key term

Home front – civilian life inside Germany during the war years

Life during the early years of the war, 1939–41

Revised

- The success of the **blitzkrieg** tactics used by the German army in Poland and western Europe brought quick victories. These secured new supplies of raw materials as well as food and luxury goods which were sent back to Germany.
- Germany followed a policy of autarky by attempting to become self-sufficient. This meant the rationing of food, clothes and fuel which was introduced in 1939. The food ration cards had the unexpected result of imposing a healthier and more balanced diet upon the German population.
- Fearing bombing raids, children were evacuated from Berlin in September 1940 but many soon returned. It was not until 1943 that mass evacuation of children took place, with Austria and Bavaria being the main destinations.
- All sections of society were encouraged to play a part in the war effort. The Hitler Youth became active in collecting metal, clothing and books for recycling.
- Although the Nazis believed a woman's place was in the home, more and more women were recruited into industry after 1937. They were needed to fill the places left by conscripted men. However, this did not become official policy until much later in the war.
- Goebbels made effective use of propaganda using the German victories of 1939–41 to boost morale at home and ensure support for the war effort.

Key term

blitzkrieg – lightning war. The new method used by the German armed forces in 1939

Life during the later war years, 1942–45

Revised

- During 1942–43 Germany suffered several key defeats such as the battles of Stalingrad and El Alamein which meant the war was no longer going in her favour.
- In a speech in February 1943 Goebbels announced the policy of **Total War**, which meant ensuring all sections of the economy and society played a part in the war effort.
- To keep up morale Goebbels launched an intensive propaganda campaign. Posters played on the fear of Communism, offering the stark choice of 'Victory or Bolshevism'.
- In September 1943 Albert Speer was appointed Reich Minister for Armaments and Production. He quickly took direct control of the war economy, cutting the production of consumer goods and concentrating upon war production. Productivity was increased and foreign workers were brought in to cover labour shortages. By 1944 29 per cent of all industrial workers were foreign.
- In 1943 the Nazis tried to mobilise women and 3 million women aged 17–45 were called to work. Only 1 million took up jobs.
- As defeats mounted, food shortages increased and in 1942 food rations were reduced. Parks and gardens in cities were dug up and used as vegetable patches. The short supply of goods led to illegal trading and a flourishing black market.
- In May 1943 Britain and the USA began a heavy bombing programme against German cities. The aim was to disrupt war production and destroy civilian morale. Berlin, Cologne, Hamburg and Dresden were all severely bombed. Millions of people were made homeless, many leaving the cities and becoming refugees. Raids on Dresden in February 1945 destroyed 70 per cent of all the buildings in the city and more than 150,000 civilians were killed in just two night attacks. Around 800,000 civilians were killed during the Allied bombing campaign.
- In September 1944 the **Volkssturm**, a people's home guard, was formed. It was to be used to defend Germany's cities against the Allied invasion. It was made up of men too old to serve in the army and boys from the Hitler Youth, who were all expected to provide their own uniforms and weapons. Its members lacked experience and were poorly trained. However, they did play an active role in the defence of central Berlin against the Russian invasion in April 1945.

Key terms

Total War – a war in which all available weapons and resources are used

Volkssturm – a German militia set up by Hitler in 1944 to recruit young and older German males to help defend Germany against Allied invasion

Revision task

Copy and complete the following table to show the differences between the two phases of the war for life on the home front in Germany.

	1939–41	1942–45
Everyday life		
Food supplies/rationing		
Evacuation/city bombing		
Total War		
Morale/propaganda		
Volkssturm/Home Defence Force		

The Nazi treatment of Jews during the war years

Revised

Following the outbreak of war in 1939, the Nazi persecution of the Jews intensified but it did not follow any mapped-out plan. The policy evolved as the needs of war dictated.

- **Emigration:** the initial solution was forced emigration and at one point the French island of Madagascar was considered as an area for the resettlement of Europe's Jews.
- **Ghettos:** rapid German success in the early stages of the war caused the adoption of a more radical policy. The invasion of Poland brought 3 million Jews under Nazi control and Jews were herded into ghettos, the largest being in Warsaw. Surrounded by a large wall, conditions within the ghettos were extremely harsh. Overcrowding and meagre rations meant that thousands died of starvation, disease and the cold weather. Around 55,000 Jews died in the Warsaw ghetto.
- **Einsatzgruppen:** following the German invasion of the USSR in June 1941 another 5 million Jews came under Nazi control. Special killing squads known as **Einsatzgruppen** moved into the USSR behind the advancing German armies to round up and shoot Jews, burying them in mass graves. By 1943 such squads had murdered more than 2 million Jews.
- **Wannsee Conference:** on 20 January 1942 leading Nazis met at Wannsee in Berlin to work out a '**Final Solution**' to the Jewish question. It was decided that death camps would be built in Poland and Jews from all over Nazi-occupied Europe would be transported there.
- **The Final Solution:** gas chambers and crematoria were built in camps at Auschwitz, Treblinka, Maidanek, Sobibor and Belzec in Poland. On arrival at these camps Jews were divided into two groups: those who were fit were forced to work to death in the labour camps; those labelled 'unfit' were sent directly to the gas chamber. Conditions within the camps were terrible. Those identified for work were fed very little food and they lived in cramped, filthy conditions where disease spread quickly. Their life expectancy was short. By the time the camps were liberated by the Allies in 1945 up to 6 million Jews and 500,000 gypsies had been worked to death, gassed or shot in what became known as the **Holocaust**.

Key terms

Einsatzgruppen – SS Special Action Squads responsible for the brutal killing of civilians in occupied territories

Final Solution – the Nazi plan for the systematic mass slaughter of Europe's Jews

Holocaust – mass slaughter, the Nazi murder of over 6 million Jews

Revision task

Make a copy of the following table. Use the information in this section to explain how and why Nazi policies towards the Jews grew harsher as the war progressed.

The treatment of the Jews during the war years, 1939–45		
Policy/action	**Why this policy/action was adopted**	**What happened to the Jews as a result of this policy/ action**
Emigration		
Ghettos		
Einsatzgruppen		
Death camps and gas chambers		

Exam practice

Explain why the Nazis introduced the Final Solution programme in 1942. **[5 marks]**

Answers online

Examiner's tip

In 'explain why' questions you need to give two or more reasons, supporting your answer with specific factual detail. In this instance you need to talk about how the Nazi invasions of Poland and the USSR brought millions of Jews under their direct control and consider the thinking behind the decisions made at the Wannsee conference in January 1942.

9.2 How much opposition was there to the Nazis within Germany during the war years?

Opposition to Nazi rule from civilians

Revised

As the war turned against Germany, resistance and opposition to the regime became more common, particularly from youth groups and religious leaders.

Opposition from young people

- **Edelweiss Pirates**: this group objected to the way the Nazis attempted to control the lives of young people. They wore check shirts and dark trousers and their emblem was the edelweiss flower. They beat up members of the Hitler Youth, pushed propaganda leaflets dropped by Allied planes through letterboxes, and sheltered deserters from the armed forces. Barthel Schink, the sixteen-year-old leader of the Cologne Pirates, together with twelve other members of this group, were hanged by the Gestapo in November 1944.
- **Swing Youth:** members tended to be middle class. They rejected the ideals of the Hitler Youth and developed a rival culture. Swing clubs were established in bars, nightclubs and houses in cities such as Hamburg, Berlin, Frankfurt and Dresden. They listened to British and American music, especially jazz.

Opposition from students

- **White Rose Group:** this was set up by Hans and Sophie Scholl and Professor Kurt Huber at Munich University in 1941. The group called for a campaign of passive resistance against the Nazi regime and distributed pamphlets to make people aware of Nazi atrocities. They painted anti-Nazi slogans on walls and on 18 February 1943 the leaders were arrested by the Gestapo for distributing anti-Nazi leaflets; they were tortured and hanged.

Exam practice

Source A: A pamphlet published by fifteen members of the White Rose Group at Munich University on 18 February 1943

'The day of reckoning has come. This is the day when German youth will get their revenge on Hitler. In the name of German youth we demand from Adolf Hitler the return of our personal freedom which he took from us. There can be but one word of action for us: Fight the Nazis. Each of us must join in the fight for our future. Students, the eyes of the German nature are upon us. The dead of Stalingrad beg us to act.'

How useful is Source A to a historian studying opposition to the Nazi regime during the Second World War? **[6 marks]**

Answers online

Examiner's tip

For the 'how useful' questions you need to make sure that your answers include reference to what the source actually says (its **Content**), that you identify who said this (its **Origin**) and that you refer to the circumstances under which it was written (its **Purpose**). This will enable you to make a judgement about whether the information is balanced or biased and if it is biased, why it is biased. Think: **COP**.

Opposition from religious groups

Once the true nature of the Nazi regime became apparent, opposition developed from individuals and groups within the Church.

- **Martin Niemöller** set up the Confessional Church in 1934 as an alternative to the National Reich Church. He frequently spoke out in public against the Nazi regime. He was eventually arrested and spent seven years in concentration camps.
- **Dietrich Bonhoeffer** was a Protestant pastor and member of the Confessional Church. He spoke out critically against Nazi racist policies and helped Jews escape to Switzerland. He was arrested by the Gestapo in October 1942 and executed in April 1945.
- **Von Galen, the Catholic Archbishop of Munster**, spoke out critically against the Nazi euthanasia policy, Gestapo terror and concentration camps. He became known as the 'Lion of Munster' but was arrested following the July Bomb Plot of 1944 (see page 86).

Opposition to Nazi rule from the military

Revised

- **General Ludwig Beck and his circle**: Beck resigned from his post in the army because he disagreed with Hitler's plans to challenge the Versailles settlement. Together with Karl Goerdeler, a Nazi official, they gathered together a circle which organised two failed assassination attempts upon Hitler's life in March and November 1943. They also played a leading role in the July Bomb Plot.

- **Colonel Claus von Stauffenberg and the July Bomb Plot, 1944**: this was the closest the German military came in attempting to assassinate Hitler.

Stauffenberg was badly wounded on the Eastern Front, losing his left eye, right arm and two fingers of his left arm. He was appalled by the atrocities he saw at the Front and became convinced of the need to remove Hitler.

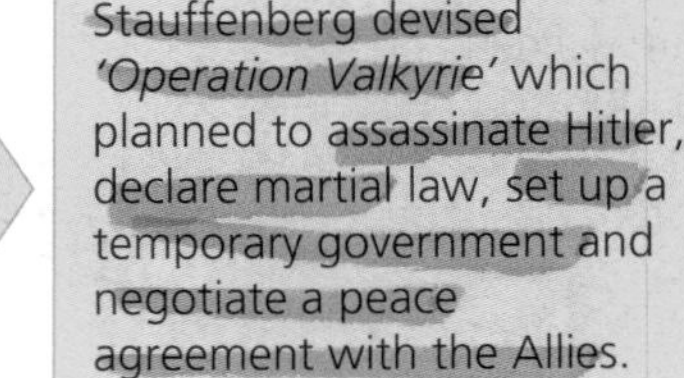

On 20 July 1944, Stauffenberg left a bomb under the table in a conference room at Hitler's headquarters at Obersalzberg in East Prussia. Making an excuse, Stauffenberg left the room before the bomb exploded. It killed four people but Hitler received only minor wounds.

Those involved in the plot were quickly hunted down. Stauffenberg was arrested in Berlin and shot. General Beck committed suicide. In total 5746 people suspected of being involved were executed, including 19 generals and 27 colonels.

On 24 July all members of the German army were required to re-swear an oath of loyalty to the Führer.

↑ **The July Bomb Plot, 1944**

Revision task

Make a copy of the following table. Use the information in this section to describe the type of opposition to Nazi rule that emerged within Germany during the war years and how it was dealt with.

Opposition to Nazi rule during the war years, 1939–45			
	Name of group/ individual	**Examples of opposition displayed by this group/ individual**	**How such opposition was dealt with by the Nazi authorities**
Young Germans			
University students			
Religious leaders			
German military			

9.3 What was the situation in Germany following total defeat in the war?

By early 1945 it was clear that Germany had lost the war. The Allies were advancing through Germany on both the Eastern and the Western Fronts and, by April, Berlin was under attack.

Developments on the Eastern Front, 1943–45

Revised ☐

- 1942–43 was the turning point in the war on the Eastern Front, when the Germans failed to take the city of Stalingrad and surrendered their forces.
- In July 1943 the Germans were defeated at the Battle of Kursk, losing 2000 tanks. The Soviet Union now began to advance westwards at a rapid rate.

- By the end of 1944 all German troops had been pushed out of the Soviet Union.
- Soviet forces liberated Warsaw in Poland on 17 January 1945, Budapest in Hungary on 11 February and Vienna in Austria on 13 April.
- By mid April 1945 Soviet forces were threatening Berlin.

Developments on the Western Front, 1943–45

Revised

- By 1943 the Germans were losing the Battle of the Atlantic and their U-boats were no longer a major threat.
- On 6 June 1944, D-Day, Allied forces landed on the Normandy beaches, opening up a second front (the Western Front) in the attack on German forces.
- After capturing the beachheads Allied forces advanced through France, liberated Paris on 25 August and pushed on into Belgium.
- In December 1944 German forces launched a counter-attack through the Ardennes (the Battle of the Bulge) and to begin with they broke through the American lines. However, they were eventually pushed back.
- Heavy bombing raids by the RAF and USAAF during 1943–45 destroyed industrial sites, roads, bridges and rail networks across Germany, causing disruption to the German war effort.
- On 9 March 1945 Allied forces crossed the River Rhine at Remagen and entered Germany, hoping to get to Berlin before the Soviets did.

Allied Forces Affects

The fall of Berlin, April 1945

Revised

- On 16 April the Soviet attack on Berlin started. It involved 1.5 million men, 6300 tanks and 8500 aircraft.
- By 24 April Berlin was surrounded and fierce house-to-house fighting took place. About 100,000 members of the Volkssturm attempted to defend the city.
- On 2 May General Weidling, the defence commandant of Berlin, ordered the surrender of German forces defending the city.
- Over 300,000 Soviet troops had been killed or wounded in the battle for Berlin.

The death of Hitler and the German surrender

Revised

- Hitler spent his last days in an underground bunker in the Reich Chancellery.
- At midnight on 28 April he married Eva Braun.
- In his political testament he left the leadership of Germany split between Admiral Dönitz and Goebbels.
- On 30 April Hitler and Braun committed suicide; afterwards their bodies were wrapped in a blanket, taken outside the bunker, soaked in petrol and burnt.
- On 1 May Goebbels committed suicide.
- On 4 May Hitler's remains were found by Soviet troops and taken away for examination.
- On 8 May Dönitz agreed to the Allied terms of unconditional surrender which ended the war and the Third Reich.

The condition of Germany at the end of the war

Revised

- Around 3.25 million soldiers and 3.6 million civilians had been killed.
- The country was swarming with refugees.
- More than 25 per cent of all homes had been destroyed.
- Almost all major towns and cities lay in ruins.
- The economy was in ruins – money was worthless and had been replaced by bartering.

Revision tasks

1. Explain the importance of each of the following events in the downfall of the Third Reich.
   - Battle of Stalingrad
   - Battle of Kursk
   - D-Day
   - Battle of Berlin
   - Death of Hitler
   - Unconditional surrender
2. Write a paragraph to describe the condition of Germany in May 1945.

The punishment of a defeated Germany

A key aim of the Allies was to prevent Germany from ever being able to threaten the peace of Europe again. Decisions about the future of Germany were made at two important conferences.

The Yalta Conference, February 1945

Revised

In February 1945 the three Allied leaders, Churchill, Roosevelt and Stalin, met at Yalta in the Crimea to consider what to do with Germany once the Nazi regime was defeated. It was decided that Germany was to be divided into four zones of occupation (British, French, American and Soviet zones). Berlin was also to be divided into these four zones. It was agreed to hunt down Nazi war criminals and to allow countries liberated from Nazi rule to have free elections to decide their future government.

The Potsdam Conference, July 1945

Revised

A second conference was held at Potsdam on the outskirts of Berlin in July. Tensions between the Allies were emerging as the Soviets showed no signs of withdrawing from Eastern Europe. The division of Germany and Berlin agreed at Yalta was confirmed and it was also agreed to demilitarise the country, ban the Nazi Party, begin the process of **denazification** and put Nazi leaders on trial.

Key term

Denazification – attempt to remove Nazi influence

The Nuremberg Trials

Revised

On 21 November 1945, 22 senior ranking Nazis and 200 other Nazis were put on trial at Nuremberg. They were charged with waging war, committing crimes against peace and humanity, and war crimes. The trials lasted until 1 October 1946, with 142 people being found guilty and 24 receiving death sentences (eleven of which were later amended to life imprisonment). Goering cheated the hangman by committing suicide the night before his execution.

Policy of denazification

Revised

This was a deliberate policy of removing traces of the Nazi regime from German society, culture, press, economy, judiciary and politics. It was achieved through a series of directives issued by the Allied Control Council and included the following actions:

- **10 October 1945** – the National Socialist Party was dissolved and its revival totally prohibited.
- **1 December 1945** – all German military units dissolved.
- **12 January 1946** – issue of criteria for the removal from public office of anybody who had played more than a nominal role in Nazi Party activities. Special courts were set up to determine the extent of involvement of Party members in the Nazi regime. However, it proved impossible to examine all Party members thoroughly and many escaped justice.
- **13 May 1946** – confiscation of all media associated with Nazism or militarism. Over 30,000 books were banned.

Germany in 1947

Revised

By 1947 the division between East and West Germany was beginning to appear. In the western zones (British, French, American) capitalism and democracy were being introduced, and in the eastern zone (Soviet) communism was emerging as the dominant force. Churchill used the phrase 'Iron Curtain' to describe the division emerging between East and West. In 1949 two separate countries were created from the occupation zones – the three western zones merged to form the Federal Republic of Germany, while the eastern zone formed the German Democratic Republic. The two countries of East and West Germany continued to exist until reunification in 1990.

Revision task

Copy and complete the chart below to show how the Allies dealt with Germany after the defeat of the Third Reich.

How the Allies dealt with Germany after the defeat of the Third Reich	
Decisions made at Yalta and Potsdam	
Nuremberg Trials	
Policy of denazification	
Situation in Germany in 1947	

Exam practice

Source A: The division of Germany and Berlin in 1948

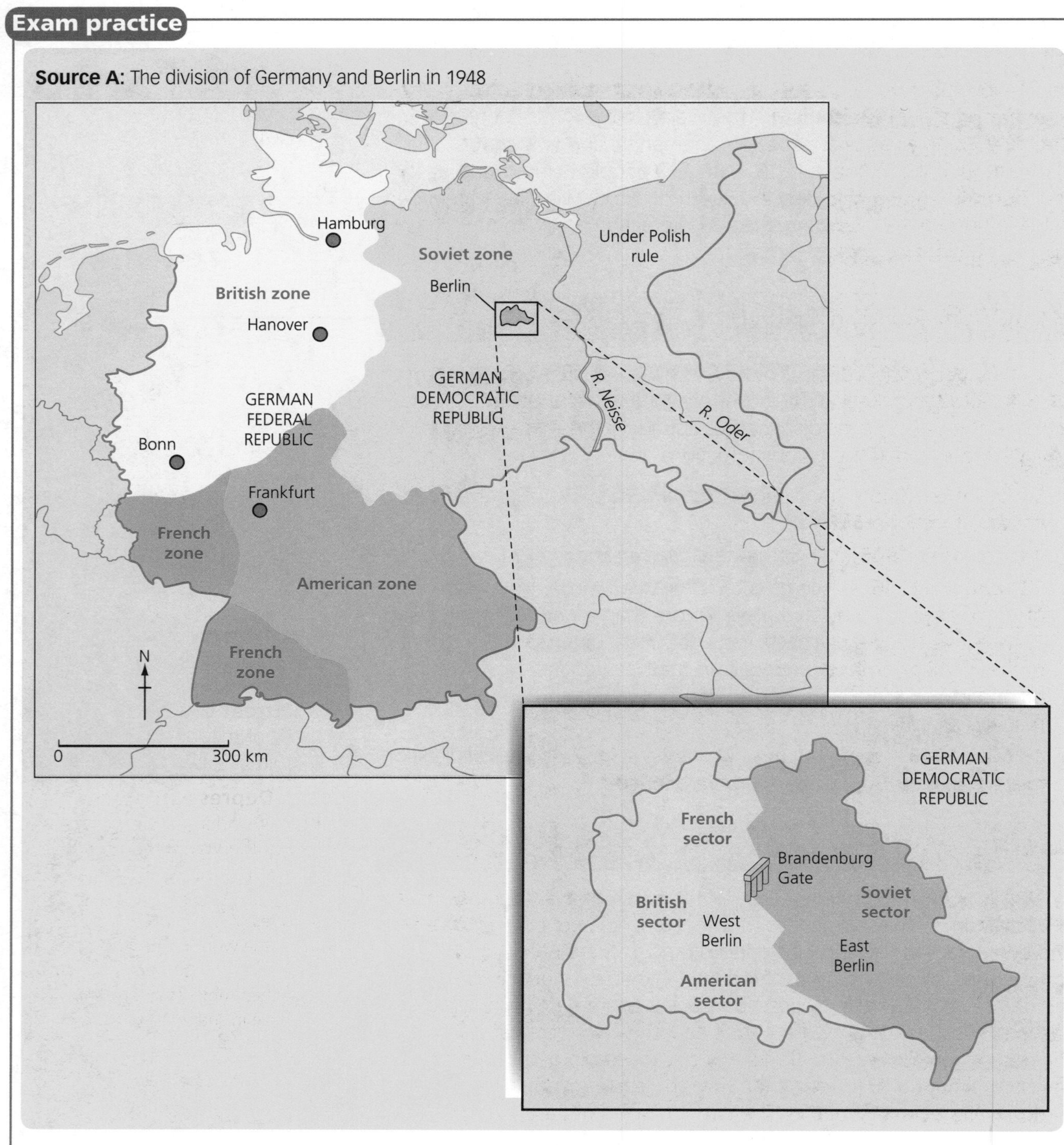

What does Source A show you about Germany after 1945? **[2 marks]**

Answers online

Examiner's tip

In this type of question you need to pick out specific detail from what you can see in the source and from the caption attached to it. In this context you need to say that the map shows that Germany was divided into zones, each controlled by an Allied power. Berlin was also divided. It is important that you *'say what you see'*.

Chapter 10 Changing life in the USA, 1929–2000

Key issues

You will need to demonstrate good knowledge and understanding of the key issues of this period. These are:

- What were the main influences on American life between 1929 and 1945?
- What were the main political and economic developments in the USA after 1945?
- What were the main social developments in the USA from 1945 to 2000?

10.1 What were the main influences on American life between 1929 and 1945?

Economic downturn

The impact of the Wall Street Crash

In October 1929 the panic selling of shares on Wall Street led to a loss of confidence in the financial markets. Share prices crashed causing the collapse of the US stock market. The event became known as the **Wall Street Crash** and it was to lead to the **Great Depression.**

Key terms

Wall Street Crash – the collapse of the American stock market in October 1929

Great Depression – the economic and social slump which followed the Wall Street Crash

Impact of the Wall Street Crash

Rising unemployment
- Factories, banks and businesses collapsed.
- Mid 1929 unemployment = 1.5 million
  1930 = 5 million
  1931 = 9 million
  1932 = 13 million

Depression in the cities
- By 1933 one-third of the workforce in the cities was unemployed.
- Many could not pay their rent and became homeless, forced to live in shanty towns called **Hoovervilles.**

Family life
- There was no system of social security so many were forced to rely on charity and handouts.
- There was a sharp rise in suicides, a fall in the number of marriages and a fall in the birth rate.

Depression in the countryside
- Many farmers were unable to sell their produce and became bankrupt.
- Many were evicted and became **hobos** searching for work.
- A drought in 1931 caused the soil in Oklahoma, Colorado, New Mexico and Kansas to turn to dust.
- Dust storms affected 20 million hectares creating a 'dust bowl'.

Key terms

Hoovervilles – shanty towns built on the edges of cities by the unemployed during the Great Depression; named after President Hoover

Hobo – an unemployed wanderer searching for work

The response by President Hoover to the Depression

Revised

Herbert Hoover was a Republican who became President in 1928. He was criticised for doing too little to help those affected by the Depression:

- He believed in balancing the budget and refused to borrow money to help create jobs.
- He believed in '**rugged individualism**'.
- In May–June 1932 the **Bonus Army** of unemployed war veterans marched on Washington to demand the early payment of war bonuses which were due to be paid in 1945. They set up a huge Hooverville outside the White House. Hoover sent in troops to remove them and burn down the shanty town.

Key terms

Rugged individualism – The idea that individuals were responsible for their own lives and should not expect help from the government

Bonus Army – First World War veterans who gathered in Washington in 1932 to demand cash payment of war bonuses

Such actions and beliefs helped to create an image of a president who did not care. It gave rise to a popular slogan: 'In Hoover we trusted, now we are busted'.

However, in 1932 Hoover did attempt to introduce measures to relieve the crisis:

Reconstruction Finance Corporation (February 1932) – this gave $2 billion of federal aid to ailing banks, insurance companies and railroads.

Emergency Relief Act (July 1932) – this gave $300 million to state governments to help the unemployed.

Home Loan Bank Act (July 1932) – twelve regional banks were set up to stimulate house building and home ownership.

These measures had little time to work before a presidential election was held in November 1932.

The 1932 presidential election

Revised

The two candidates fighting the presidential election in November 1932 were the Republican Herbert Hoover, who was attempting to be re-elected, and the Democrat Franklin Delano Roosevelt (FDR). Roosevelt won a landslide victory, securing 42 of the 48 states.

Key term

New Deal – policies introduced by President Roosevelt to deal with the effects of the Great Depression

Republican candidate: Herbert Hoover	Democrat candidate: Franklin Delano Roosevelt
Hoover was deeply unpopular: • Republicans were blamed for the Depression • Hoover was criticised for the harsh treatment of the Bonus Army • Relief schemes were too small and too late • Hoover seemed to offer nothing new.	Roosevelt possessed attractions: • Democrats offered a more caring image • Roosevelt had overcome personal hardship: he suffered from polio – he was a fighter • Roosevelt kept his message simple – the 'three R's' (see page 93) • He promised the American people a '**New Deal**'.

Revision tasks

1. Using your knowledge of this topic, explain the impact of the Great Depression on:
   a) unemployment
   b) city dwellers
   c) farmers.
2. Give three reasons why Hoover lost and three reasons why Roosevelt won the 1932 presidential election.

Roosevelt and the New Deal

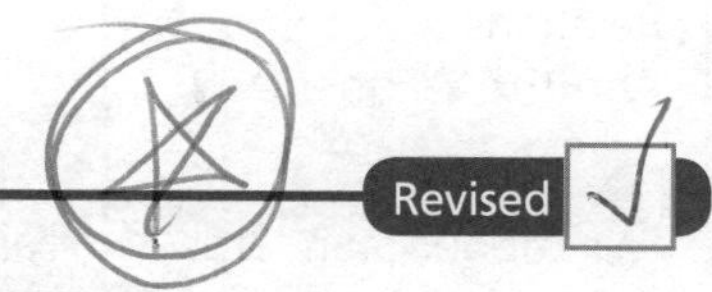

When he took office as President in January 1933 Roosevelt introduced a change of policy known as the New Deal. It was based upon the 'three R's' – Relief, Recovery and Reform. In his first hundred days (9 March–16 June 1933) he introduced a large number of government programmes aimed to restore the shattered economy. In so doing he created the **Alphabet Agencies**.

Key term

Alphabet Agencies – nickname given to the group of organisations set up as part of the New Deal

The First New Deal		
Legislation/Agency	**Problem**	**Solution/Action taken**
Emergency Banking Act **(EBA)**	Americans had little confidence in the banks; many banks had gone bankrupt	The government closed all banks for ten days; Roosevelt reassured the American people that their money was safe; the government officially backed 5000 banks which helped to restore confidence.
Federal Emergency Relief Administration **(FERA)**	Poverty and unemployment	This provided $500 million for emergency relief to help the poor and homeless, e.g. providing food and clothing.
Civilian Conservation Corps **(CCC)**	Unemployment among young people	This provided six months of work for men aged between 18 and 25 in conservation projects such as planting trees to stop soil erosion; by 1940 over 2 million men had been given work in the CCC.
Public Works Administration **(PWA)**	Unemployment	The government spent $3,300 million on public works projects for the unemployed – slum clearance; building schools; roads; hospitals.
Agricultural Adjustment Administration **(AAA)**	Rural poverty, low crop prices	This was intended to help farmers increase their profits; subsidies were paid to farmers to destroy their crops and slaughter animals in an effort to push up prices; by 1936 farm incomes were one and a half times higher than in 1933.
National Industrial Recovery Act **(NIRA)**	Poor economic condition of the USA	This led to the setting up of the National Recovery Administration (NRA) to encourage employers to improve conditions; it introduced codes of practice for minimum wages, hours and conditions; companies complying with the code could display the Blue Eagle symbol.
Tennessee Valley Authority **(TVA)**	Agricultural over-production; regular flooding in the Tennessee Valley	A huge public works programme was set up to build 21 dams to irrigate the land and generate hydroelectric power; farmers were given loans and training in soil conservation.

In January 1935 Roosevelt introduced a Second New Deal which targeted the rights of workers, the poor and the unemployed.

The Second New Deal		
Legislation/Agency	**Problem**	**Solution/Action taken**
Works Progress Administration **(WPA)**	Unemployment	This oversaw job creation schemes – putting people to work building roads, schools, hospitals, airports, harbours.
National Labour Relations Act (the Wagner Act)	Workers' rights	This gave workers the legal right to join trade unions; it stopped employers sacking union members; it set up the National Labour Relations Board which protected workers against unfair practices.
Fair Labour Standards Act	Fair play for workers	This tightened up laws against child labour and minimum wages; 300,000 workers secured higher wages as a result and 1 million had a shorter working week.
Social Security Act	Poverty	This set up a national system of social security, providing pensions for the over 65s and aid to the disabled, widows and orphans, as well as unemployment benefits.

Revision task

For each of the following Alphabet Agencies, write out its full name and describe what it did to help tackle the problems caused by the Great Depression: CCC, AAA, TVA, EBA, PWA.

Successes and criticisms of the New Deal

Revised

Successes of the New Deal

The New Deal helped to restore confidence and faith in government; it stimulated the economy and put the country back on its feet:

- America avoided the swing to Communism and fascism that overtook Europe.
- Millions of jobs were created through the Alphabet Agencies – 4 million people were employed on public works schemes created by the PWA and WPA; 2.5 million were employed in the CCC.
- The TVA improved the lives of 7 million people.
- The income of farmers doubled between 1932 and 1939 as a result of the AAA.
- The New Deal stabilised the US banking system and restored confidence to the markets.
- Workers were protected by codes of practice and trade unions were allowed.
- It created a semi-Welfare State, providing pensions for the elderly and widows, and state help for the sick, disabled and unemployed.

Criticisms of the New Deal

1. Some believed the New Deal did not go far enough:

- The New Deal agencies discriminated against black people; they either got no work or received lower wages than white workers.

- Huey Long, governor of Louisiana, criticised Roosevelt for not sharing out the nation's wealth fairly and proposed his own 'Share Our Wealth' campaign.
- Father Charles Coughlin criticised the New Deal for not doing enough to help the needy; his weekly radio broadcasts attracted over 40 million listeners.
- Dr Frances Townsend argued that Roosevelt had not done enough to help old people and proposed a pension of $200 a month for everyone over 60.

2. Some believed that the New Deal undermined important American values, principles and laws:

- Some felt that the federal government now interfered too much in the affairs of the American people; the New Deal went against the belief in rugged individualism.
- It was argued that the new social welfare measures encouraged people to live off the state.
- Republicans were highly critical, claiming that Roosevelt was changing the accepted role of government in the USA.
- Many viewed trade unions as un-American as they were seen to take away the right of choice from workers.
- Some conservative Democrats were critical, believing that too much power was given to trade unions.
- In 1935 the Supreme Court ruled that the NRA was unconstitutional, and in 1936 it declared the AAA unconstitutional, claiming that Roosevelt had used federal powers which the constitution had not given him.

3. Later historical reflections have concluded that:

- the Alphabet Agencies were short-term solutions that provided cheap labour and did not solve the underlying economic problems.
- unemployment did fall but it was America's entry into the Second World War in 1941 that ultimately lifted the country out of the Depression.

Revision tasks

1. Which do you think are the three most important successes of the New Deal?
2. Which are the three strongest criticisms?

Exam practice

How important was President Roosevelt to the lives of the American people in the 1930s? **[8 marks]**

Answers online

Examiner's tip

In the 'how important' questions you need to identify 2–3 key reasons why something was important, using specific factual detail to back up your comments. In this instance you should refer to how Roosevelt restored confidence to the financial sector, how his New Deal created jobs and stimulated the economy and how this impacted upon the lives of American people.

The impact of the Second World War on the US economy and society

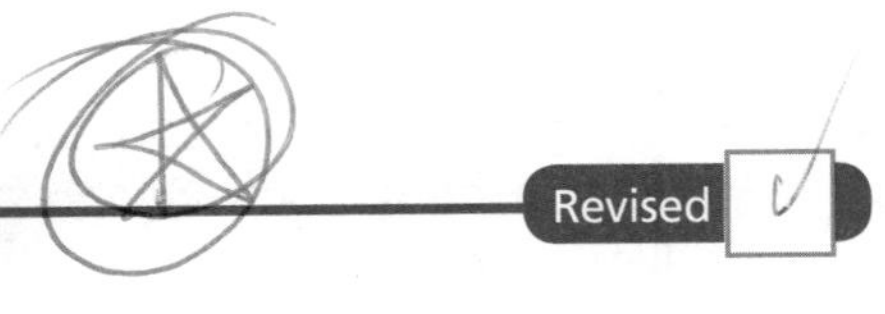

War had broken out in Europe in 1939 but America did not enter the conflict until after the Japanese bombing of Pearl Harbor in December 1941.

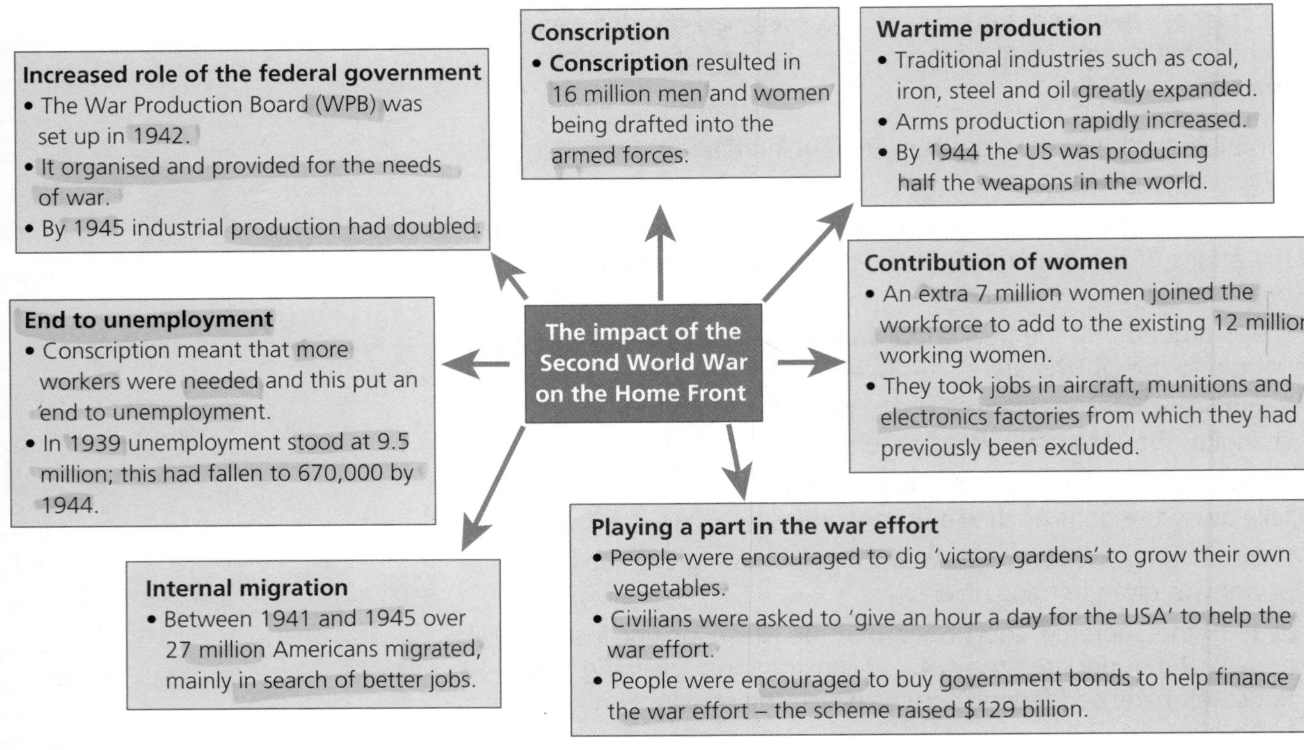

Key term

Conscription – compulsory military service of men aged 18–45

10.2 What were the main political and economic developments in the USA after 1945?

The development of the affluent society in the 1950s

Following the death of President Roosevelt in April 1945, the new President, Harry S. Truman, introduced a programme of economic development and social welfare which became known as the '**Fair Deal**'. The policy was continued by his successor, President Dwight Eisenhower, and it led to the prosperity of the 1950s.

Key terms

Fair Deal – the domestic policies of President Truman, 1945–53

Suburbia – the residential area on the outskirts of a city

Affluence – a time of increasing wealth and prosperity

Reasons for the growth of suburbia

Affordable housing
- The building of reasonably priced houses became a priority.
- Land was cheaper on the edges of cities.

Baby boom
- Between 1945 and 1960 the population increased by 40 million.
- This increased the demand for new homes.

Living the American Dream
- The dream of many young couples was to own their own home.
- They also wanted to bring their children up away from the pressures of city life.

Increasing car ownership
- Most families had at least one car.
- This meant they no longer had to live close to their place of work.

Increasing affluence
- Economic growth led to people having more money to spend.
- It made the new homes affordable.
- They could afford the new appliances such as televisions and record players.

Life in suburbia

During the 1950s many middle-class families moved away from the centre of cities to new homes in the suburbs. Here they could live the 'American Dream' of owning their own home furnished with the latest 'must have' household appliances.

While the 1950s was a time of growing prosperity from which many Americans benefited, it was not a time of affluence for all.

Key terms

Ghetto – part of a city inhabited by a minority because of social and economic pressure

Affluence for all?	
The Affluent Society	**The 'Other' America**
• By 1960 the standard of living of the average American was three times that of the average Briton. • By 1960 25 per cent of Americans lived in suburbia. • Television sets, record players, swimming pools and at least one car became status symbols, the 'must have' items.	• By 1959 29 per cent of the population (50 million) lived below the poverty line. • Included among the poor were the 'hillbillies' of the Appalachian mountains; Hispanic workers in the west; black people in the city **ghettos** in the north. • Poor Americans found it hard to afford the rising cost of healthcare (there was no national health service).

Revision task

Write a paragraph to describe the key features of life in suburbia in 1950s America.

The Red Scare and McCarthyism

In the years after 1945 the USA experienced a **Red Scare** which led to a movement known as **McCarthyism**.

Key term

Red Scare – anti-Communist hysteria in the USA

McCarthyism – the practice of making accusations of disloyalty or treason without proper evidence

Cold War – a war of nerves and mutual distrust between the USA and USSR from 1945 to 1991

The Red Scare 1945–50

- This was largely the result of the onset of the **Cold War** and the expansion of Communism into Eastern Europe after the Second World War. In 1949 China also turned Communist and between 1950 and 1953 the Korean War was fought to stop the spread of Communism. Many felt that Communist ideas were infiltrating American society.
- The Federal Bureau of Investigation (FBI) was led by an anti-Communist director, J. Edgar Hoover. Between 1947 and 1950, 3 million government employees were investigated by the FBI for Communist links.
- In 1947 the House of Un-American Activities Committee (HUAC) in the US Congress investigated the 'Hollywood Ten' (Hollywood writers, producers, directors) for Communist links. The Hollywood Ten refused to answer questions under interrogation and were jailed for one year.
- In 1948 Alger Hiss of the US State Department was investigated as a suspected Communist.
- In 1951 Julius and Ethel Rosenberg were found guilty of spying (on flimsy evidence) for the USSR and were executed.

McCarthyism

- In 1950 Joseph McCarthy, a young Republican Senator, claimed he had the names of 205 Communists who were working in the State Department.
- As Chairman of a Senate Committee, McCarthy began to investigate Communist activities in the government, interviewing hundreds of individuals.
- Throughout 1952 and 1953 McCarthy extended his investigations – he investigated libraries for anti-American books written by Communists; he targeted high-profile figures and accused them of Communist activities, often on little evidence.
- Thousands of lives were ruined by this 'witch-hunt'. It led to people being blacklisted which meant they could not find work. Over 100 university lecturers were fired and 324 Hollywood personalities were blacklisted.

never produced evidence

The end of McCarthyism

- In 1954 McCarthy accused 45 army officers of being Communist agents.
- McCarthy was challenged and asked to produce evidence to support his accusations.
- The Army–McCarthy hearings were televised – McCarthy was seen to be rude, abusive and bullying in his manner.
- McCarthy's popularity fell dramatically and his 'evidence' was exposed as no more than rumours.
- He was dismissed from office and died an alcoholic in 1957.
- McCarthyism showed the extent of anti-Communist feeling in America and brought great suffering to those who had been accused.

Revision task

Use your knowledge of this topic to write three bullet points under each of the following headings:

- Reasons for McCarthyism
- Key events of McCarthyism
- Reasons why McCarthyism died out

Kennedy's 'New Frontier' (1961–63)

Revised

In November 1960 John F. Kennedy, a Democrat, was elected President. He introduced a programme of reform called the '**New Frontier**' which aimed to tackle three focus areas: poverty, inequality and deprivation.

Key term

New Frontier – the reform policies of President Kennedy in the early 1960s

The New Frontier	
Civil Rights	Kennedy appointed Thurgood Marshall as America's first black federal judge; he sent troops to ensure that James Meredith could be the first black student at Mississippi University; he introduced a Civil Rights Bill.
Economy	Kennedy introduced a $900 million public works programme to build roads and public buildings; he increased spending on defence and space technology which created jobs; he cut taxes to encourage people to buy goods.
Social Reform	Kennedy proposed introducing Medicare – a cheap system of state health insurance; the Social Security Act 1962 gave financial help to the elderly and unemployed; the Area Redevelopment Act 1961 gave loans and grants to states with long-term unemployment; the Housing Act 1961 gave cheap loans for redevelopment of inner cities.

However, Kennedy faced opposition in Congress to his ideas and many of his bills were rejected. He was assassinated in November 1963 and so was unable to complete his reform programme.

Johnson's 'Great Society' (1963–68)

Revised

Kennedy's successor as President, Lyndon B. Johnson, decided to continue with the reform programme and develop it further. Johnson's '**Great Society**' declared war on poverty, aiming to make America a country with high living standards and a sense of community.

Key term

Great Society – the reform programme of President Johnson in the 1960s

The Great Society	
Civil Rights	The Civil Rights Act 1964 banned discrimination and set up the Equal Opportunities Commission; the Voting Rights Act 1965 ensured fair voting procedures; in 1967 the ban on mixed marriages was lifted.
Economy	Johnson cut taxes to encourage people to spend, help businesses grow and create jobs; he improved the railways and highways; he gave federal funds to help depressed areas such as the Appalachians.
Social Reform	The Medical Care Act 1965 provided Medicare (for the old) and Medicaid (for the poor); the Elementary and Secondary Education Act 1965 provided the first ever federal funding for state education; the Model Cities Act 1966 targeted urban renewal and slum clearance; the minimum wage was increased; funding was provided for education and community projects in inner cities.

Like Kennedy, Johnson faced powerful opposition in Congress to his reform measures. However, following Kennedy's assassination the American people were more sympathetic to the reforms he had wanted for the US, and Johnson was an experienced politician able to win support for such measures.

Revision tasks

1. Copy and complete the table below to show how Presidents Kennedy and Johnson attempted to deal with the three key issues of poverty, inequality and deprivation.

	What the New Frontier did to tackle this key issue	**What the Great Society did to tackle this key issue**
Poverty		
Inequality		
Deprivation		

2. Who achieved most in their efforts to improve American society – Kennedy or Johnson? List the reasons for your choice.

Political and economic developments from the 1970s

The Watergate scandal and its consequences

Revised

In 1968 Richard Nixon, a Republican, was elected President and was re-elected in 1972. He promised to end America's involvement in the Vietnam War and to cut federal government expenditure.

Key term

Impeachment – to bring the US President to trial for treason

In August 1974 Nixon was forced to resign as President because of the Watergate scandal which had begun in 1972:

- In 1972 Nixon set up CREEP – Committee to Re-elect the President – giving permission to use any tactics.
- On 17 June 1972 five members of CREEP were arrested for breaking into the Watergate offices of the Democratic Party.
- Nixon ordered a cover-up and denied any knowledge of the incident and went on to win a landslide re-election victory.
- In January 1973 the Watergate burglars went on trial and were all convicted. Nixon again denied any cover-up.
- On 30 April 1973 Nixon's top advisers Bob Haldeman and John Ehrlichman resigned.
- On 25 June 1973 Nixon's sacked lawyer, John Dean, testified to the Senate Watergate Committee that there had been a cover-up directed by Nixon.
- It was revealed that all the President's conversations had been taped but Nixon refused to hand over the tapes.
- On 21 November 1973 the tapes were handed over but some were missing or contained gaps.
- On 30 April 1974 Nixon was forced to hand over all the tapes unedited which showed that he had repeatedly lied throughout the investigation.
- On 27 July 1974 Congress decided to **impeach** Nixon.
- On 8 August 1974 Nixon resigned to avoid impeachment.
- On 6 September 1974 President Gerald Ford pardoned Nixon for his part in the scandal.

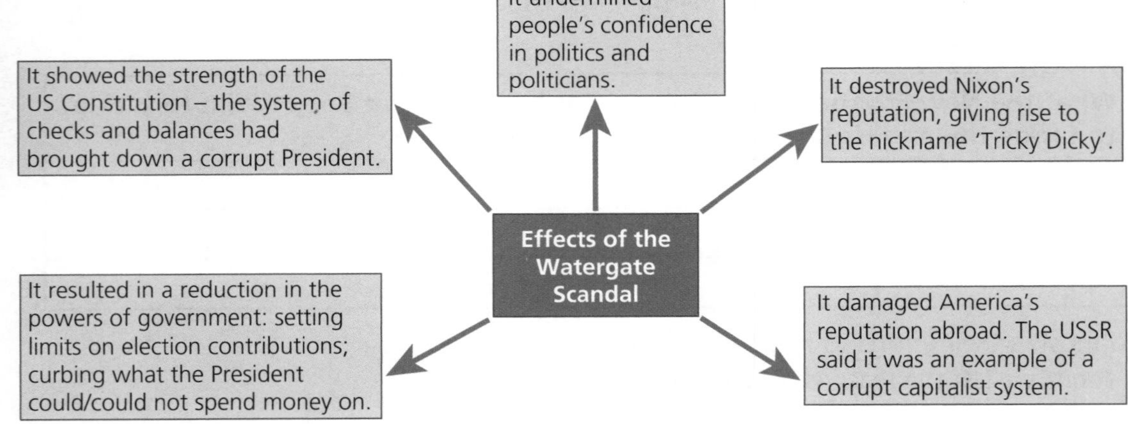

Revision task

Make a copy of the following table. Use your knowledge of the Watergate scandal to complete each section.

Key events of the Watergate break-in and trial	Reasons for Nixon's resignation	Key effects of the Watergate scandal

The domestic policies of Presidents Reagan, Bush Snr (senior) and Clinton

Revised

US Presidents, 1974–2000		
Gerald Ford	1974–1977	Republican
Jimmy Carter	1977–1981	Democrat
Ronald Reagan	1981–1989	Republican
George H. Bush Snr	1989–1993	Republican
Bill Clinton	1993–2001	Democrat

The policies of Ronald Reagan

- In 1980 Reagan defeated Jimmy Carter to become President. He inherited severe economic problems – high inflation (15 per cent); rising unemployment (7.5 per cent); high **budget deficit**; world recession.
- Reagan introduced a series of economic reforms which obtained the nickname **'Reaganomics'**.
- He slashed income tax (cutting taxes by $33 billion, the largest tax cut in US history), hoping to encourage people to spend and thereby create jobs.
- He slashed welfare programmes by $20 billion a year for three years, returning to the ideal of 'rugged individualism'.
- He cut taxes at a time when government expenditure increased (especially on the space programme) and this caused the **national debt** to grow.
- 1987 saw the worst stock market crash since 1929 and the US began to edge into recession.

Key terms

Budget deficit – when a government spends more money than it receives through taxes and has to borrow

Reaganomics – the economic policies of President Reagan in the 1980s

National debt – money owed by the government

The policies of George Bush Snr

President Bush Snr continued with Reagan's domestic polices but he faced severe economic problems:

- The budget deficit had trebled in size between 1980 and 1990.
- Bush was forced to go back on election promises and increase indirect taxes and impose new taxes on the wealthy.
- The budget deficit continued to grow – in 1992 it was calculated that 14 per cent of all Americans lived in poverty.
- Bush did pass two important acts in 1990 – a Disability Act which forbade discrimination based on disability and a Clear Air Act.
- There were serious race riots in 1992 in Los Angeles, Atlanta, Birmingham, Seattle and Chicago.

The policies of Bill Clinton

Unlike Reagan and Bush Snr, Clinton was a Democrat who promised more direct action from the federal government to tackle the country's economic problems. There were three key features to his domestic policies:

- **Abandon Reaganomics** – he increased federal government spending, increased taxes and reduced the national debt – policies which helped to bring sustained economic growth.
- **Welfare reforms** – in 1996 he introduced a minimum hourly wage; his Health Security Bill which aimed to set up a system of universal health insurance was rejected by Congress.
- **Scandals** – an investigation into the Whitewater scandal of 1996 revealed that Clinton had been having an affair with Monica Lewinsky, a former member of the White House staff. He was threatened with impeachment.

Revision task

Make a copy of the following table. Use your knowledge of the domestic policies of Presidents Reagan, Bush Snr and Clinton to complete each section.

	Response of President Reagan to:	**Response of President George Bush Snr to:**	**Response of President Clinton to:**
Taxation			
Government expenditure			
Welfare programmes			

Exam practice

Describe President Reagan's domestic policies in the 1980s. **[4 marks]**

Answers online

Examiner's tip

When answering 'describe' questions you need to ensure that you include 2–3 key factors. To obtain maximum marks you need to support them with specific factual detail, in this instance describing the key features of 'Reaganomics' – slashing taxes, cutting welfare programmes, a return to rugged individualism.

10.3 What were the main social developments in the USA from 1945 to 2000?

There were major changes to US society in the second half of the twentieth century, partly resulting from the impact of the cinema, television, music and developments in information technology.

Changes in popular culture

The cinema and movie stars

Revised

After its significant popularity in the inter-war period, the cinema lost some its appeal from the 1950s onwards, mostly due to the rise in television ownership. However, there were some notable achievements for the cinema:

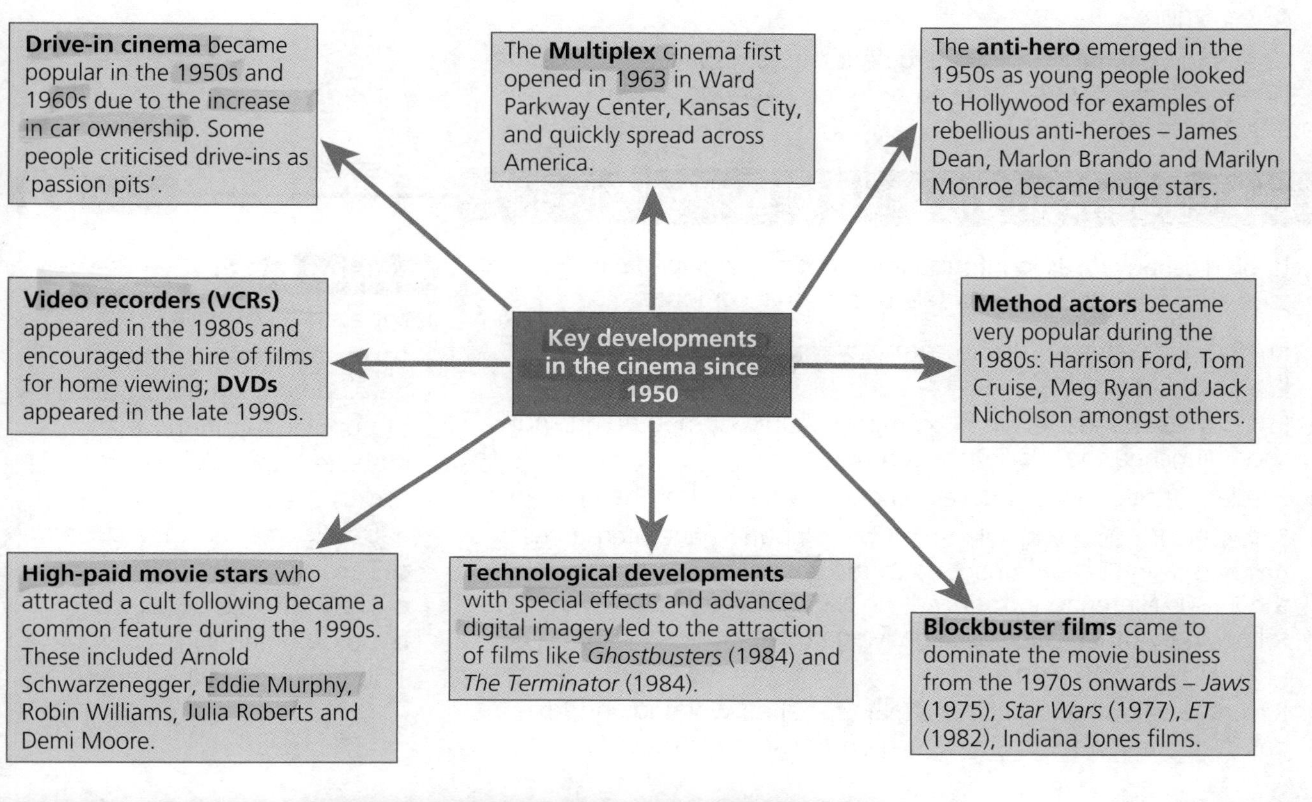

The motor car

Revised

The growth in car ownership in the 1950s and 1960s helped the development of popular culture:

1945	25 million Americans owned cars
1960	60 million Americans owned cars

1960	61 million cars in America = one car for every three people
1970	89 million cars in America = one car for every two people

- The car helped to open up the suburbs of towns and cities.
- The car helped to open up the countryside, allowing Americans to explore their country.
- In 1955 Disneyland in Southern California opened – 40 per cent of visitors came from outside California, mainly by car.

The influence of television

Revised

Television quickly established itself as an important feature in American society:

- The number of televisions increased from 7000 in 1946 to 50 million in 1960 and by 1970, 96 per cent of US households had at least one television.
- TV personalities became household names, such as Lucille Ball who appeared in the popular comedy 'I Love Lucy'.
- During the 1950s and 1960s the 'western' genre became very popular, especially series programmes such as *The Lone Ranger*, *Bonanza* and *Gunsmoke*.
- By the 1980s soap operas had taken centre stage, the most popular being *Dallas* (1978–91), *Dynasty* (1981–89) and *Beverly Hills 90210* (1990–2000).
- Chat shows came to attract large audiences, especially the *Oprah Winfrey Show* (1986–2011) and the *Jerry Springer Show* (1991–present).

Developments in information technology

Revised

Technological advances in information technology helped cause a massive growth in the use and sale of personal computers:

- In 1975 Bill Gates set up his company Microsoft and in 1985 he launched Microsoft Windows.
- In 1976 Steve Jobs set up his company Apple Computer Inc and soon launched the Macintosh computer.
- The late 1990s saw the development and growth of the internet.
- Since the 1980s the development of computer-generated games has had a significant impact upon the younger generation – in the 1980s Nintendo introduced the NES game console which was followed by others such as Sega Mega Drive, Sony PlayStation and in 2001 Microsoft Xbox.
- Recent developments such as email, social networking and text-based discussion forums have helped transform US society.

Revision task

For each factor give **three examples** of how developments in that aspect of popular culture have impacted upon American society:

- Developments in the cinema
- The motor car
- The influence of television
- Developments in information technology

Changes in youth culture

One of the greatest social changes in the USA in the 1950s and 1960s was the emergence of a distinct youth culture.

The 1950s – emergence of the teenager and teenage rebellion

Revised

- The teenager of the 1950s had more money and free time than ever before.
- Many seemed to want to rebel, especially against whatever their parents believed in.
- Some rebellious teens wore distinctive clothes, formed gangs, cruised in cars, drank heavily and attacked property; those who dropped out of conventional society became known as **beatniks**.

Key term

Beatniks – anti-conformist youths of the 1950s

- Some were influenced by writers of the 1950s who questioned the cosy values of suburbia, such as J D Salinger in his novel *The Catcher in the Rye* (1951) which dealt with a high school dropout.
- Many teenagers were influenced by youth films of the 1950s such as *Rebel Without a Cause*, which made a cult hero of James Dean who played a young man who rebelled against his parents and got into trouble with the police for drunken behaviour.
- The development of rock and roll music gave teenagers their own brand of music. In 1956 Elvis Presley exploded onto the pop music scene; his songs *Heartbreak Hotel* and *Hound Dog* broke all sales records.
- Stars like Presley and Little Richard became heroes to a new youth culture. Many parents disliked Presley's energetic dancing and upfront sexuality.

The 1960s – the hippy movement

Revised

- During the 1960s many young people rejected their parents' lifestyles and values.
- Some young people 'dropped out' of society and became **hippies** – they wore ethnic style clothes, grew their hair long, took drugs like marijuana and LSD recreationally, followed mystical religions and engaged in 'free love'.
- Hippies opposed the Vietnam War, wore flowers in their hair as a symbol of peace, and the slogan 'Make love, not war' became common.
- They settled in communes and San Francisco became the hippy capital of America.
- The high point of the movement was the Woodstock rock concert in August 1969, attended by half a million hippies; rock groups like The Grateful Dead and The Doors exerted a powerful influence.

Key term

Hippy – an individual who rejects conventional social standards in favour of universal love and fellowship; the hippy movement developed in the USA in the mid 1960s

The 1970s to 2000 – developments in popular music

Revised

- The 1970s witnessed the rise of disco music through such performers as Donna Summer, the Bee Gees and the Jacksons. The film *Saturday Night Fever* (1977) witnessed the height of disco fever.
- Rap and hip hop music developed out of the disco music of the 1970s and was a product of inner-city problem areas with high unemployment amongst young black Americans.
- During the 1990s artists/bands such as Jay-Z, Ice-T, Will Smith and the Fugees all achieved great chart success.

Revision task

Use the information in this section to help you describe the key characteristics of each of the following periods.

- 1950s: teenage rebellion
- 1960s: hippy movement
- 1970s to 2000: developments in popular music

Student protest and its impact

Revised

During the 1960s students became heavily involved in various protest movements:

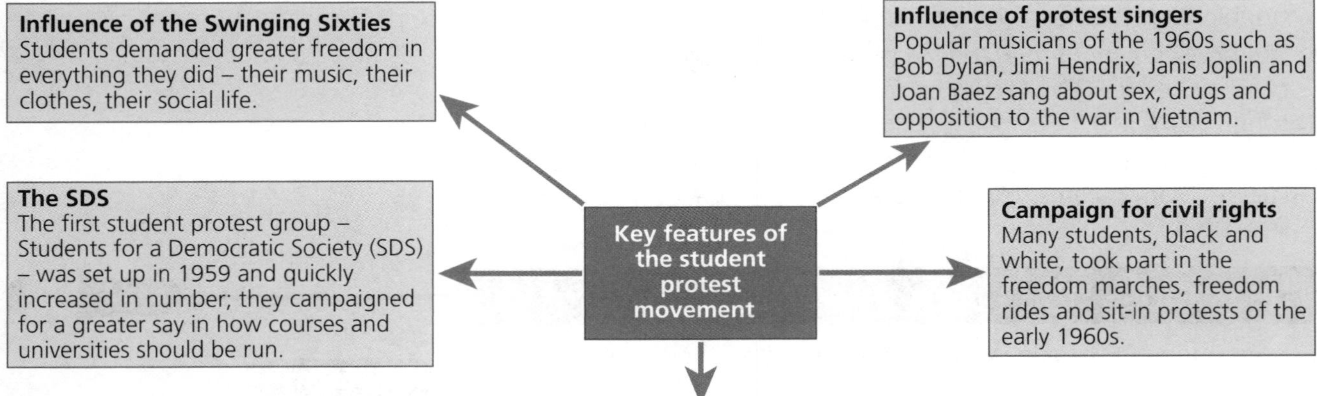

Anti-war protests

- Many students protested against the 'draft system' which called them up to fight in Vietnam.
- Anti-war protests reached a peak during 1968–70; in 1969 700,000 people marched in Washington DC against the war, with students burning their draft cards and the US flag.
- Student protests at Kent State University in May 1970 resulted in National Guardsmen shooting dead four student protestors.

The changing role of women in the USA

There were important changes in the position of women in US society in the second half of the twentieth century.

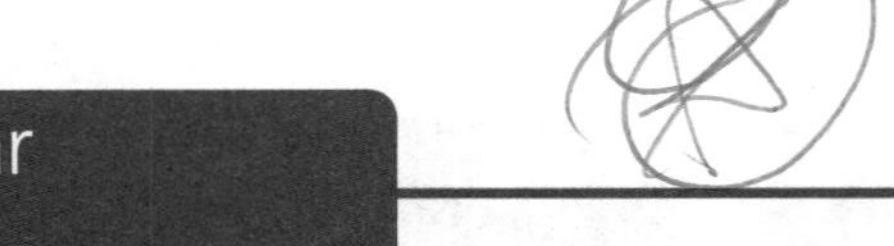

The impact of the Second World War and the 1950s

Revised

The impact of the Second World War

- The Second World War increased employment opportunities for women: 6 million women entered factories in traditional 'male' jobs as machinists and toolmakers; 300,000 joined the armed forces.
- After the war the majority of women gave up their wartime jobs and returned to their roles as mothers and wives, or to their traditional 'female' jobs in teaching, nursing and secretarial work.

The 1950s

- The media exerted influence in encouraging women to adopt their traditional family role.
- Boredom with the domestic routine and increased freedom due to labour-saving devices encouraged some women to seek paid employment, although the choice of career was very limited.

The growth of the feminist movement – the 1960s and 1970s

Revised

- In 1950 women made up 29 per cent of the workforce; by 1960 this had risen to 50 per cent.
- A government report published in 1963 revealed that women earned only 50–60 per cent of the wages of men who did the same job; it showed that 95 per cent of company managers were men and only 7 per cent of all doctors and 4 per cent of all lawyers were women.
- In 1963 Betty Friedan published *The Feminine Mystique* which ridiculed the common belief that women were only suited to low-paid jobs and called for progress in female employment opportunities.
- In 1966 Friedan and others set up the National Organisation for Women (NOW) which demanded equal rights for women and challenged discrimination in the courts; by the early 1970s it had 40,000 members.
- More radical than NOW was the Women's Liberation Movement which became more active in challenging discrimination; it attracted publicity through **feminists** burning their bras in public and in 1965 they picketed the Miss America beauty contest.
- Changes in the law helped to secure more equality:
  - the Civil Rights Act (1964) banned discrimination due to gender
  - in 1973 abortion was legalised, giving women more freedom of choice.

Key term

Feminist – a person who believes in equal social, economic and political rights for women

The growth of the feminist movement – 1980 to 2000

Revised

- During the last two decades of the twentieth century women broke into traditionally male-dominated careers:
  - in 1981 Sandra Day O'Connor became the first woman to be appointed to the US Supreme Court
  - in 1983 Dr Sally Ride became the first American woman to enter space on the shuttle *Challenger.*
- By 1995, 70 per cent of women of working age were in employment, compared with only 38 per cent in 1955.
- However, many of these jobs were in traditional female occupations and by 1998 women's earnings were about 75 per cent of those of men.

1955 = 38%
1995 = 70%.

Exam practice

Use Sources A and B and your own knowledge to explain why life had changed for some women in the USA by the 1960s. **[6 marks]**

Source A: An American housewife in the 1950s

Source B: From a school history text book

'By the mid 1960s there were 1.5 million women at university. This suggests that many women were becoming increasingly bored and frustrated with life in comfortable suburbia.'

Answers online

Examiner's tip

In this type of question you need to identify 'change' or 'lack of change', making direct reference to the information in both sources linked to your knowledge of this topic area. In this instance you should mention that Source A projects a stereotypical image of a suburban housewife of the 1950s which is in contrast to Source B which shows women of the 1960s breaking out of the housewife mould and taking up careers outside the home. **Tip:** remember to spell out the change and the reasons for it.

Chapter 11 Changing attitudes to the race issue in the USA, 1929–2000

Key issues

You will need to demonstrate good knowledge and understanding of the key issues of this period. These are:

- Why was there so much racial inequality in the USA between 1929 and 1945?
- Why was it difficult for black Americans to gain equal rights in the USA in the 1950s and 1960s?
- How much progress has been made by black Americans since the 1960s?

11.1 Why was there so much racial inequality in the USA between 1929 and 1945?

The position of black people in the 1930s

Segregation and the 'Jim Crow' laws

Revised 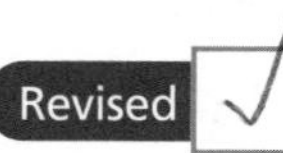

In the south

In the states of the Deep South (e.g. Arkansas, Mississippi, Georgia) there was strict **segregation**. This was imposed through the **'Jim Crow' laws** which segregated black people in schools, parks, hospitals, swimming pools, libraries, restaurants, cinemas and on public transport. Black people were prevented from voting or had to pass literacy or other tests to do so. The Scottsboro trials of 1931 showed the injustice when eight black boys were convicted of raping two white females on very circumstantial evidence.

Key terms

Segregation – keeping a group separate from the rest of society, usually on the basis of race or religion

'Jim Crow' laws – laws which introduced segregation and discrimination against black Americans in the southern states

In the north

Northern states such as Michigan and New York did not have segregation laws but racism was still commonplace. During the 1920s thousands of black workers migrated from the south to cities like Chicago, Detroit and Pittsburgh in search of work. It was known as the Great Migration. They were given low-paid jobs and tended to live in squalid tenement ghettos.

However, there were improvements for some. Jazz brought fame to black singers and musicians such as Louis Armstrong. The black neighbourhood of Harlem in New York became the centre of the Harlem Renaissance for black singers, musicians, artists, writers and poets.

The NAACP

Revised 

- Formed in 1909 by William Du Bois, the NAACP was active in fighting against racial injustice throughout the 1930s and 1940s, mostly using the legal system.

- During the 1920s it had campaigned against lynching and was the main opponent of the Ku Klux Klan.
- In 1930 the NAACP successfully blocked the nomination of Judge John Parker, a known racist, to be appointed to the Supreme Court.
- During the war the NAACP pressured Roosevelt into ordering a non-discriminatory policy in war-related industries and federal employment.
- The NAACP employed the black lawyer Thurgood Marshall to fight against segregation in education; he secured equal salaries for teachers.
- Through pressure from the NAACP, the Supreme Court ruled that blacks had the right to the same quality of graduate education as whites.

Revision tasks

1. List four ways in which black Americans were treated as second-class citizens during the 1930s.
2. Construct a spider diagram to show the work of the NAACP during the 1920s and 1930s in its fight against segregation.

The Ku Klux Klan

Revised

- Founded at the end of the Civil War in the mid 1860s, the KKK was a racist organisation which believed in white supremacy.
- Its members had to be WASPS (White, Anglo-Saxon, Protestants) and they were anti-Communist, anti-Jewish, anti-Catholic and against all foreigners.
- Klansmen dressed in white robes and white hoods to symbolise white supremacy and also to conceal their identity.
- They used terror and violence to intimidate anybody who supported equal rights – acts of intimidation included cross-burning, beatings, mutilations, castration, tar and feathering and lynching.
- The Klan was strong in the southern states and membership reached a peak of nearly 6 million in the mid-1920s, but a scandal surrounding the prosecution of a Klan leader, David Stephenson, in 1925 caused a sharp fall in membership; by 1930 membership stood at just 30,000.
- The Klan had a powerful grip on how many southern states were run – its members included police officers, lawyers and judges; many politicians in the south knew that if they opposed the Klan they might not be elected to Congress.
- Despite its decline in members the Klan remained active and powerful; in 1946, 15,000 people marched to the Lincoln Memorial in Washington to demand that the organisation be made illegal.

The impact of the Depression and the New Deal

After the Wall Street Crash of 1929 America entered into the Great Depression of the 1930s. Black people suffered badly, being *'the last to be hired, the first to be fired'*:

- By 1932 one-third of all black males were jobless.
- Two million black farmers and sharecroppers had been forced off the land.
- Unemployment among blacks in the northern cities was 60 per cent.
- Three times as many black families claimed relief as whites in the southern states during the Depression.

Roosevelt's 'New Deal' programme did not bring radical changes for black Americans but it did bring about some improvement in their economic condition:

- The New Deal provided 1 million jobs for black Americans and training for 500,000.
- The Public Works Administration (PWA) allocated funds for the building of black hospitals, universities and housing projects.
- The Federal Emergency Relief Administration (FERA) granted aid to 30 per cent of all black American families.
- The number of black Americans employed by the government rose from 50,000 in 1933 to 200,000 in 1945.

However, Roosevelt did little to eliminate unfair hiring practices and job discrimination. He also failed to support anti-lynching bills.

Revision task

Use your knowledge of this topic to identify **three** factors showing the impact of the Depression on the lives of black Americans. Now identify **three** improvements in the lives of black Americans brought about by the New Deal.

Black people and the Second World War

The Jim Crow Army

Revised

Following America's entry into the war in 1941 many black Americans enlisted. They had to fight for their country in segregated units.

- In the army there were black-only units which formed the **Jim Crow Army**.
- Before 1944, black soldiers were not allowed into combat in the marines – they were used only to transport supplies or as cooks and labourers.
- The navy would only accept blacks as mess men (working in the canteens).
- The US air force would not accept black pilots until the formation of an African American 332nd Fighter Group known as the Tuskegee airmen; by the end of the war there were 1000 black pilots.
- The 761st Tank Battalion, nicknamed the 'black panthers', saw action in the Battle of the Bulge in France and Belgium in 1944.

Key term

Jim Crow Army – a segregated unit of the US army made up of black Americans which fought in the Second World War

In 1948, as a direct consequence of the contributions of black Americans to the war effort, President Truman banned 'separate but equal' recruiting, training and service in the army, air force, navy and Marine Corps.

Contribution to the war effort on the Home Front

Revised

Black workers made an important contribution to the war effort at home:

- In 1941, fearing race riots, President Roosevelt set up a Fair Employment Practices Committee which banned discrimination against black Americans in those factories used by the government in the production of war goods.
- This was an important victory in the campaign for equality.
- By 1944 nearly 2 million black people were working in war factories.
- Black Americans began a 'Double V' campaign – victory over fascism abroad and victory over discrimination at home.
- Membership of the NAACP rose from 50,000 to 450,000 during the war.

The impact of the war on the civil rights issue

In 1946, as part of his 'Fair Deal' programme, President Truman set up a civil rights committee. This proposed an anti-lynching bill and the abolition of the requirement that black Americans had to prove they had paid tax in order to be able to vote. Due to opposition, Truman was unable to implement these recommendations. However, Truman's support for civil rights gave encouragement to the NAACP which began to challenge the segregation laws in the courts in the 1950s.

Exam practice

Why was the Second World War a turning point for black Americans? **[8 marks]**

Answers online

Examiner's tip

This type of question on 'turning points' requires you to spell out why a particular event resulted in change. In this instance you need to refer to the experience of black Americans in the war effort both at home and overseas, and how this gave them encouragement and determination to challenge the segregation laws. **Tip:** remember to concentrate on the reasons 'why'.

11.2 Why was it difficult for black Americans to gain equal rights in the USA in the 1950s and 1960s?

There was considerable progress in the campaign for improved civil rights during the 1950s and 1960s, particularly in the attempts to remove segregation from education and public transport.

The struggle for equal education

Brown v. Topeka Board of Education, 1954

Revised

- In 1952, 20 US states had segregated public schools.
- Linda Brown had to walk 20 blocks to her school in Topeka, Kansas, even though there was a school for white pupils just a few blocks from her home.
- In 1952 her father, Oliver Brown, with the help of the NAACP, took the Board of Education to court.
- After losing the case in the state courts, the NAACP took the case to the Supreme Court.
- In May 1954 the Supreme Court ruled that racial segregation in public schools went against the US constitution.
- However, the Supreme Court had no power to impose its decision and many southern states continued to ignore the ruling.

Little Rock Central High School, Arkansas, 1957

Revised

- In September 1957, nine African-American students led by Elizabeth Eckford attempted to enter the white-only Central High School in Little Rock.
- The Governor of Arkansas, Orval Faubus, surrounded the school with National Guardsmen to prevent the nine students from entering.

- President Eisenhower responded by sending 1000 federal troops of the 101st Airbourne Division to protect the students for the rest of the school year.
- Eight of the nine students graduated at the end of the year.
- Little Rock is important because it showed that the President could and would enforce court orders with federal troops and it brought publicity to the injustices of segregation.
- However, by 1964 fewer than 2 per cent of African-American children attended multi-racial schools in the southern states.

James Meredith and Mississippi University, 1962

Revised

- In June 1962 the Supreme Court upheld a federal court decision to force Mississippi University to accept the black student James Meredith.
- When Meredith arrived to register for admission he was prevented from doing so by the Governor of Mississippi.
- Riots broke out and President Kennedy sent in 2000 troops to restore order.
- 300 soldiers had to remain on the university campus to protect Meredith until he graduated with his degree three years later.

Revision task

For each of these events, identify the reasons for the dispute, the court decision and the importance in the campaign to secure equality in education:

- Brown v. Topeka
- Little Rock
- Meredith and Mississippi University

The struggle for equality in public transport

The Montgomery bus boycott, 1955–56

Revised

This took place in Montgomery, Alabama, and is considered to mark the beginning of the civil rights movement.

- In Montgomery a local law stated that African Americans had to sit on the back seats of buses and had to give up those seats if white people wanted them.
- On 1 December 1955 Rosa Parks, an NAACP activist, refused to give up her seat and was arrested and convicted of breaking the bus laws.
- Local civil rights activists set up the Montgomery Improvement Association (MIA), led by the Reverend Dr Martin Luther King, a young Baptist minister. The group organised a boycott: they deliberately stopped using the buses, arranging private transport for people.
- Civil rights lawyers fought Rosa Parks' case in court and in December 1956 the Supreme Court declared Montgomery's bus laws illegal. The bus company gave in.
- This was the beginning of non-violent mass protests by the civil rights movement.

Non-violent direct protest gathers pace – sit-in protests

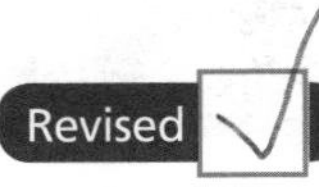

Revised

In the winter of 1959–60 civil rights groups stepped up their non-violent campaigns. They organised marches, demonstrations and boycotts to end segregation in public places. In February 1960 in Greensboro, North Carolina, the **sit-in** protests began at the lunch counter in the F. W. Woolworth store. By August 1961 the sit-ins in restaurants, libraries and movie theatres had attracted over 70,000 participants and resulted in over 3000 arrests.

Key term

Sit-in – a form of protest in which demonstrators sit in a public place and refuse to move

The 'freedom rides', 1961

Revised 

- Segregation still existed on interstate buses and in May 1961 members of the Congress of Racial Equality (CORE) began a form of direct protest in the southern states known as the 'freedom rides'.
- They deliberately rode on buses run by companies that were ignoring laws banning segregation. The first freedom rides began at Washington DC on 4 May 1961 with the plan of travelling down to New Orleans – once they reached the southern states the riders met with a hostile reception.
- At Anniston, Alabama, a bus was attacked and burnt. In Montgomery, white racists beat up several freedom riders. At Birmingham there was no police protection for the freedom riders and they were attacked by an angry mob. In Jackson, Mississippi, 27 freedom riders were jailed for 67 days for sitting in the whites-only section of the bus station.
- The freedom riders continued, against much violence, throughout the summer. By September 70,000 students had taken part and 3600 had been arrested.
- The Attorney General Robert Kennedy was able to get the Interstate Commerce Committee to end segregation in all bus and rail stations and airports.

Revision task

Explain how each of the following protest strategies helped in the campaign to achieve civil rights:

- Bus boycotts
- Freedom rides
- Sit-ins

Key figures in the campaign for civil rights

The role and significance of Martin Luther King

Revised

The dominant figure in the campaign for civil rights was the Reverend Dr Martin Luther King, minister of the Dexter Avenue Baptist Church in Montgomery, Alabama.

Role and significance of Martin Luther King

Beliefs and methods
King's ideas were based on non-violent civil disobedience. He thought violence was wrong and favoured sit-ins, boycotts, freedom rides and marches as a way of protesting.

Bus boycott, 1955
King became the leader of the Montgomery Improvement Association and played a key part in the Montgomery bus boycott.

Southern Christian Leadership Conference
The SCLC grew out of the bus boycott and was formed and led by King. He was a gifted public speaker and he quickly became the leading figure in the civil rights movement.

Assassination
King was assassinated in Memphis in April 1968 by a white racist, James Earl Ray.

Birmingham march, 1963
The SCLC challenged the city of Birmingham's decision to close its public recreation facilities in order to avoid de-segregation. It organised sit-ins and marches. The protestors faced water-cannon, dogs and baton charges. King was arrested and sent to jail. President Kennedy sent in troops and Birmingham was forced to de-segregate.

Selma to Birmingham marches, March 1965
Protest marches demanding voting rights led to marchers being attacked by police and state troopers. King was sent to jail. It resulted in the passing of the Voting Rights Act (1965).

Nobel Peace Prize, 1964
This was awarded for King's work as a peacemaker, promoting non-violence and equal treatment for different races.

March on Washington, August 1963
On the steps of the Lincoln Memorial, King delivered his 'I have a dream' speech to a crowd of 250,000. It put pressure on President Kennedy to draft legislation. The Civil Rights Act was passed in 1964.

The role and significance of Malcolm X

Revised

Malcolm Little was the son of an African-American Baptist preacher who was murdered by white supremacists. In 1952 he joined the Nation of Islam and changed his surname to 'X'. He rejected King's peaceful methods and believed violence could be justified to secure a separate black nation. He was a good public speaker who attracted support from young blacks. In 1964 he left the Nation of Islam and formed the Muslim Mosque Inc and the black nationalist Organisation of Afro-American Unity. He encouraged the self-esteem of black Americans and his views and ideas became the foundation for the radical movements Black Power and the Black Panthers. He was shot dead by three members of the Nation of Islam in February 1965.

Stokely Carmichael, the Black Power Movement and the Black Panthers

Revised

- The Black Power movement emerged out of the anger and frustration expressed by young black Americans over high unemployment and poverty; its leading spokesperson was Stokely Carmichael.
- In 1966 Carmichael became chairman of the SNCC (Student Non-violent Coordinating Committee).
- He wanted blacks to have pride in their heritage and adopted the slogan 'Black is beautiful'.
- In 1968 Carmichael joined the Black Panthers, a party formed in 1966 by Bobby Seale and Huey Newton; its members wore uniforms and were prepared to use force to achieve their aim of a socialist society.
- In the 1968 Mexico City Olympics two black athletes, Tommie Smith and John Carlos, both members of the Black Panthers, used their medal ceremony to wear a single black glove and to give the clenched fist salute – it gave the movement international publicity.

Revision task

For each of the following individuals list their aims and beliefs, the methods they used to achieve equal rights for black Americans and their importance in the campaign:

- Martin Luther King
- Malcolm X
- Stokely Carmichael

11.3 How much progress has been made by black Americans since the 1960s?

Civil rights legislation

Revised

During the 1960s legislation appeared which attempted to remove discrimination and secure civil rights.

Civil rights legislation	
Civil Rights Act, 1964	• Racial discrimination banned in employment • Black students given equal rights to enter all public places and bodies receiving government money, including schools • Equal Employment Opportunities Commission set up to investigate complaints of discrimination
Voting Rights Act, 1965	• Stopped racial discrimination over the right to vote • Ended literacy tests
Supreme Court ruling, 1967	• Supreme Court ruled that state laws banning interracial marriages were unconstitutional
Fair Housing Act, 1968	• Made racial discrimination illegal in the property market

Race riots

Revised

Despite the introduction of civil rights legislation, the anger and frustration of many young blacks over continued racial injustice, high unemployment and poverty resulted in the outbreak of a series of riots across many US cities during the late 1960s.

- August 1965: riots in the Watts district of Los Angeles resulted in 34 deaths, 1072 people injured, 4000 arrests, and $40 million of damage.
- During the summer of 1969 there were riots in 125 cities across the USA.
- July 1967: riots in Newark left 26 dead and over 1000 injured.
- July 1967: riots in Detroit left 40 dead and resulted in 7000 arrests.
- President Johnson ordered an enquiry and the Kerner Report (1968) concluded that racism was deeply embedded in American society.

Exam practice

Describe the Civil Rights legislation of the 1960s. **[4 marks]**

Answers online

Examiner's tip

When answering 'describe' questions you need to ensure that you include 2–3 key factors. To obtain maximum marks you need to support them with specific factual detail, in this instance describing the key features of the Civil Rights Act, the Voting Rights Act and the Fair Housing Act.

Developments in education and housing

Revised

By the early 1990s black Americans had secured improvements in the quality of their education and housing but they still had some way to go to secure equality:

- 68 per cent of black Americans left school with a high school diploma, compared with 81 per cent of whites.
- The number of black Americans with university degrees had grown to 12 per cent of the population, compared with 22 per cent for whites.
- 85 per cent of black Americans lived in the suburbs of major cities, many in ghetto areas with poorer quality housing.
- The unemployment rate for black Americans (14 per cent) was more than twice that for whites (6 per cent).

The extent of change and progress

Revised

Since the civil rights movement of the 1960s black people have played a more active part in American society. Some have been the first Americans to achieve an award or position and these individuals have opened the door for others to follow. However, the extent of change and progress has been very uneven, and many black Americans remain among the poorest and least educated sections of US society. Frustration at continued racism was the cause of riots across Los Angeles in 1992 following the beating up of Rodney King, a black American, by police while they were arresting him.

The extent of black success in American society between the 1960s and 2000

Revised

Significant achievements by black Americans	
Politics	● 1967: Carl Stokes became the first black elected mayor of a major US city. ● 1968: Shirley Chisholm became the first black woman elected to Congress. ● 1984: Reverend Jesse Jackson made a bid for the Democratic Party's presidential nomination. ● 1989: Colin Powell became the first black American to become Chairman of the Joint Chiefs of Staff.
Sport	● In the 1960s Muhammad Ali emerged as World Heavyweight boxing champion, winning the title three times. ● Carl Lewis won nine Olympic gold medals for athletics, four of them in the 1984 Los Angeles Olympics. ● In tennis Venus Williams won the singles gold medal and doubles gold with her sister Serena in the 2000 Olympic games. ● In 1997 Eldrick 'Tiger' Woods became the first black American to win the Masters golf tournament.
Television	● In the 1980s and 1990s television produced many black stars, including Gary Coleman in *Diff'rent Strokes* and Will Smith who starred in *The Fresh Prince of Bel-Air.* ● Oprah Winfrey has dominated the 'chat show' scene and has become a role model for black American women.
Cinema	● The last 30 years have produced many black stars, including Eddie Murphy, Samuel L. Jackson, Morgan Freeman and Whoopi Goldberg. ● Spike Lee became an influential film director who revolutionised the role of black talent in Hollywood.
Music	● Black Americans have made enormous contributions to the development of popular music. ● The Tamla Motown record label launched groups and individuals such as the Supremes, the Four Tops, Stevie Wonder and the Jackson Five. ● Michael Jackson's album *Thriller* (1982) became the biggest-selling album of all time. ● More recently, black Americans have developed hip hop and rap music through artists such as Ice-T.

Exam practice

What have been the most important factors in bringing about change in the lives of black Americans since 1929?

[10 marks + 3 marks for SPaG]

Answers online

Revision task

Consider the degree of progress made by the black population in American society between 1970 and 2000, by giving three examples of 'limited progress' and three examples of 'significant progress'.

Examiner's tip

In this type of 'synoptic' essay question you need to examine the reasons for change across the years 1929–2000, making sure you cover the whole period. In this instance you need to refer to the importance of the Second World War, the campaigns for equality in education and transport in the 1950s, the civil rights movement and activists in the 1960s and political, economic and social developments since 1970. **Tip:** do not stop with the civil rights laws of the 1960s – go right up to 2000!

Chapter 12 The USA and the wider world, 1929–2000

Key issues

You will need to demonstrate good knowledge and understanding of the key issues of this period. These are:

- How and why did US foreign policy change between 1929 and 1945?
- How and why was the USA involved in the Cold War?
- What role has the USA played in the search for world peace since 1970?

12.1 How and why did US foreign policy change between 1929 and 1945?

The policy of isolationism

Revised

In the 1920s the US helped Europe recover from the First World War by:

- lending money to European countries
- taking the lead in disarmament meetings to try to prevent war in the future.

The Great Depression then strengthened arguments that America should focus on economic recovery at home and stay out of problems elsewhere in the world – **isolationism**. However, as the 1930s went on, events occurred outside the US that again demanded American involvement.

Key term

Isolationism – the belief that America should not play an important role in world problems and concentrate on what is happening in her own country

Increasing involvement in world affairs

Revised

- Roosevelt was concerned about the rise of fascist dictatorships in Europe and with Japan's expansion in China but his priority was solving economic problems at home.
- Roosevelt encouraged economic co-operation with other nations through his 'Good Neighbour Policy' which was successful in developing trade links with Latin America.
- During the late 1930s Congress passed a series of Neutrality Acts which were intended to keep America out of future wars. These banned loans and the sale of munitions to countries involved in war. However, the Fifth Neutrality Act (1939) did allow the President to authorise the **'cash and carry'** export of arms and munitions to countries at war.

Key term

'Cash and carry' – countries could buy war material from the USA provided they paid cash and transported the goods in their own ships

Concern over events in Europe – increasing US involvement

Revised

When war broke out in Europe in September 1939 Roosevelt announced that the USA would not get involved. Opinion within America was divided:

- The Committee to Defend America (CDA) was set up in 1939; it supported Roosevelt's desire to help Britain, short of going to war.
- The American First Committee (AFC) was set up in 1940; it opposed anything that might risk America's neutrality.

However, it proved difficult to avoid increased involvement in the war:

- In 1940 Congress increased the budget for defence spending and Roosevelt introduced peacetime conscription for all men aged 21–35.
- In March 1941 Congress passed the '**Lend-Lease** Agreement' which meant that America would 'lend' Britain up to $7,000 million worth of weapons; the agreement was extended to the USSR after it was attacked by Germany in June 1941.
- In August 1941 Roosevelt and Churchill agreed the Atlantic Charter which became the origin of the United Nations and set goals for a post-war world.
- During 1941 US destroyers began to escort convoys of British merchant ships as far as Iceland.

Key term

Lend-Lease – a 1941 agreement whereby America lent military equipment to Britain (and later the USSR) free of charge

Concern over Japan – deteriorating relations

Revised

- During the 1930s Japan embarked upon an expansionist foreign policy to obtain extra land and resources for its fast-growing population.
- When Japan invaded Manchuria in 1931 and northern China in 1937 the USA supported the League of Nations in condemning the actions but took no other measures.
- In September 1940 Japan joined with Germany and Italy in the Three Power Pact, a move which heightened American fears.
- Roosevelt responded by exerting economic pressure – US trading agreements with Japanese companies were cancelled; the sale of planes, chemicals and iron was stopped and in 1941 oil supplies were stopped.

Revision task

'During the 1930s America remained isolationist and refused any involvement in world affairs.' How far do you agree with this statement? List your arguments in favour and your arguments against.

America's involvement in the Second World War

The attack on Pearl Harbor – America enters the war

Revised

- On Sunday 7 December 1941 a Japanese force of 360 torpedo planes and destroyers attacked the US naval fleet at Pearl Harbor in Hawaii.
- The attack resulted in the death of 2345 US servicemen and 57 civilians; 4 battleships and 2 destroyers were sunk, 188 aircraft were destroyed and 155 were damaged.
- The US Pacific Fleet was crippled, but four aircraft carriers had not been in port that day.
- On 8 December the USA and Britain declared war on Japan.
- On 11 December Germany and Italy declared war on the USA, honouring their military agreement to help Japan.

America's involvement in the war in Europe

Revised

Roosevelt and Churchill agreed that the priority in the war was the defeat of Germany:

- In November 1942 – as Operation Torch – US and British troops began to invade Algeria, Morocco and Tunisia; by May 1943 the Germans had been defeated in North Africa.
- In July 1943 US troops invaded Sicily and in September the Italian mainland.
- On 6 June 1944 – D-Day (Operation Overlord) – 156,000 US and British troops landed on five Normandy beaches to open up a second front against Germany; the US landed 23,250 men on Utah beach, 34,250 on Omaha beach and 15,500 airborne troops were flown in; there were 2499 US D-Day fatalities.
- The Allies liberated Paris in August 1944 and pushed on into Germany; during the Battle of the Bulge (December 1944–January 1945) 19,000 US troops were killed and 60,000 were wounded.
- On 8 May 1945 Germany surrendered, ending the war in Europe.

America and the war in the Pacific

Revised

- Following Pearl Harbor, Japanese forces swept over south-east Asia and the islands of the Western Pacific.
- **By mid 1942** the Japanese had conquered over 2.5 million square kilometres of land and secured three-quarters of the world's natural rubber reserves, two-thirds of the tin reserves and vital oil supplies.
- **May 1942:** Japan experienced her first defeat by America at the Battle of the Coral Sea.
- **June 1942:** the Battle of Midway proved a turning point in the Pacific War – the Japanese failed to capture Midway Island.
- **December 1943:** following victory at the Battle of Guadalcanal, US troops captured the Soloman Islands after a four-month struggle.
- **October 1944:** the Battle of Leyte Gulf – the largest sea battle in history; the Japanese lost four aircraft carriers and two battleships and were unable to prevent the loss of the Philippines; by February 1945 US troops had captured Manila.
- **February 1945:** the island of Iwo Jima was captured by the US with the loss of 4000 US marines and 20,000 Japanese soldiers.
- **April 1945:** US troops invaded the island of Okinawa; 100,000 Japanese troops and 12,000 US troops died during a three-month fight for the island.
- **April–August 1945:** US bombing campaign using B29 Superfortress bombers; despite tremendous damage the Japanese government refused to surrender.

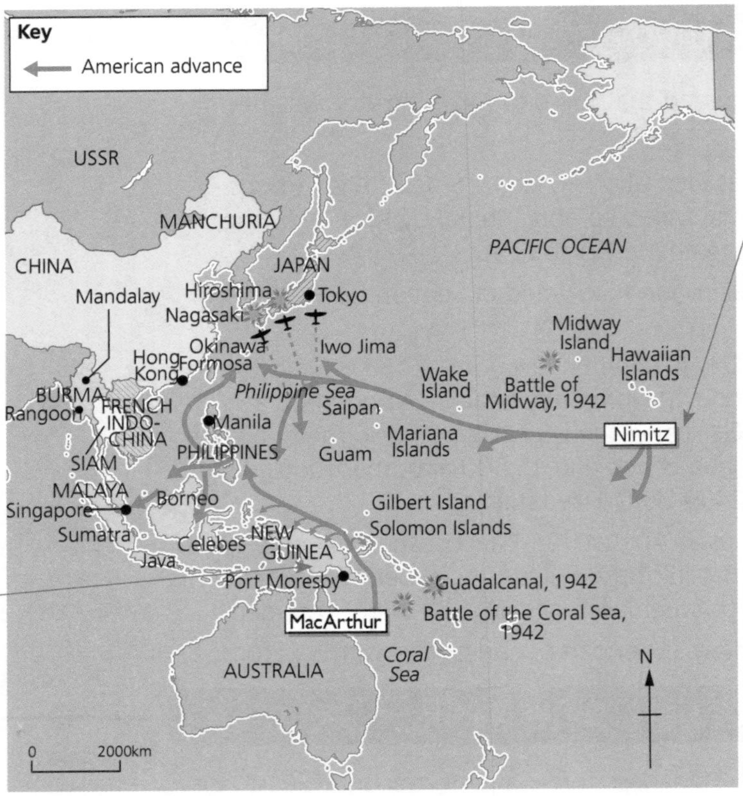

In 1942 and 1943, US General MacArthur advanced to the Solomon Islands after the successful capture of Guadalcanal.

US Admiral Nimitz led the seaborne attack westwards across the Pacific. His strategy was called 'island hopping' as he tried to recapture the chain of islands captured by the Japanese. Instead of attempting to invade every island, the USA left some alone, and therefore isolated Japanese garrisons.

↑ **Source A: Map showing American advances in the Pacific, 1942–45**

Exam practice

What does Source A show you about America's war in the Pacific?

[2 marks]

Answers online

Examiner's tip

In this type of question you need to pick out specific details from what you can see in the source and from the caption attached to it. In this context you need to say that the map shows the movement of US forces across the Pacific between 1942 and 1945, listing key battles and bombing raids. It is important that you *'say what you see'*.

The dropping of the atomic bomb

Revised

- On 6 August President Truman authorised the dropping of an atomic bomb on Hiroshima; it killed 80,000 people (the figure rose to 138,000 as a result of radiation sickness); still the Japanese would not surrender.
- On 9 August a second atomic bomb was dropped, this time on Nagasaki; it killed 40,000 (rising to 48,000 due to radiation sickness).
- On 15 August Emperor Hirohito announced Japan's unconditional surrender, ending the war in the Pacific.

Reasons for the US victory in the Pacific

Revised

- The US had a large industrial base and was able to produce more military hardware and weapons than Japan.
- Japan's industrial production was badly affected by US bombing raids.
- Key naval victories (the battles of Coral Sea, Midway and Leyte Gulf) gave the US command of the sea and air.
- The bombing of Japan's cities in 1945 destroyed one-quarter of all housing, making 22 million people homeless.

Revision task

Construct your own timeline to record America's involvement in the Second World War from 1939 to 1945. Record key events in her involvement in the war in Europe above the dateline and her involvement in the war in the Pacific below the line.

12.2 How and why was the USA involved in the Cold War?

The origins of the Cold War

Despite their political and economic differences, the USA and USSR had worked together during the Second World War to fight a common enemy, Germany. Once Germany was defeated in May 1945 relations between the two **superpowers** began to deteriorate. The result was the development of a '**cold war**' which was to last from 1945 to 1991.

Key terms

Superpowers – the term used to describe the USA and USSR which were so powerful in military and economic terms that they had left all other countries behind

Cold War – state of hostility between the USA and USSR and their allies without actual fighting

The reasons for the Cold War

Revised

- The US believed in capitalism and feared the spread of Communism.
- By May 1945 Soviet forces occupied large parts of Eastern Europe – Stalin did not intend to withdraw his troops and imposed communist-style governments upon six **satellite states** (Poland, Romania, Bulgaria, Czechoslovakia, Hungary and East Germany).
- President Truman distrusted Stalin and only informed him about America's development of an atomic bomb eleven days before it was dropped; he also made it clear that the secrets were not to be shared.
- When the leaders of the **Big Three** met at Potsdam in late July 1945 relations were strained; while they agreed that Germany was to be divided and Berlin likewise, Stalin was in no mood to allow the holding of free elections in his zones.

Key terms

Satellite states – countries under the domination of a foreign power

Big Three – the leaders of the three most powerful Allied powers: USA, USSR and Great Britain

The US policy of containment

Revised

In March 1946 in a speech at Fulton, Missouri, Churchill spoke of an '**iron curtain**' which had descended between the Soviet-controlled Eastern Europe and the free democratic states of Western Europe. It was a division that was to last until the early 1990s.

The Truman Doctrine of Containment (1947)

In March 1947 President Truman offered help to any government threatened by 'internal or external forces' in the hope of preventing any further spread of Communism. Truman's speech marked a turning point in US foreign policy – the USA was now going to be proactive in enforcing the policy of **containment**.

The Marshall Plan (1947)

Truman backed up his policy of containment with economic aid to Europe. US Secretary of State George C. Marshall offered over $13 billion in aid to countries recovering from the effects of war. Truman believed that countries with a strong economy would be able to repel Communism. Stalin refused to allow Soviet satellite states to accept **Marshall Aid**. By 1953 the USA had provided $17 billion in Marshall Aid.

Key terms

Iron curtain – term used by Winston Churchill to describe the imaginary barrier between East and West Europe

Containment – using US influence and military resources to prevent the expansion of Communism into non-Communist countries

Marshall Aid – US programme of financial and economic aid given to Europe after the end of the Second World War

The Domino Theory

Containment was based on the 'Domino Theory', the belief that if one country fell to Communism this would trigger the fall of its neighbouring countries. America's policy was to ensure that the most unstable domino did not fall.

The USA and the Cold War in Europe

The main flashpoints of the Cold War in Europe concerned attempts by the West to contain the threatened spread of Communism.

The Berlin blockade and airlift, 1948–49

Revised

Look back at the map on page 90 of this book, showing the division of Germany and Berlin, to help you revise this topic.

- After the Second World War Germany was split into four zones, each one occupied by an Allied power (USA, USSR, Britain and France). Berlin, deep in the Soviet zone, was divided in the same way.
- By June 1948 the American, British and French zones had merged together and a new currency had been introduced in an attempt to make West Germany economically prosperous.
- Stalin became increasingly worried that West Berlin would become a wealthy capitalist base within Communist Eastern Europe.
- On 24 June 1948 Soviet troops cut off all links (road, rail, canal) between West Berlin and West Germany.
- Stalin hoped the West would be forced to give up their sectors but Truman was determined to follow his policy of containment.
- The West organised an airlift to fly in supplies to West Berlin – the airlift lasted until May 1949 when Stalin gave in and re-opened all routes to West Berlin.
- Truman saw this flashpoint as a success for his policy of containment.

The USA joins NATO, 1949

Revised

The Berlin crisis had convinced Truman of the need to contain the spread of Communism and for this reason the USA joined with eleven other western powers to form the North Atlantic Treaty Organisation (NATO) in April 1949. Although a defensive alliance, its main purpose was to prevent Soviet expansion. It was the first time in its history that the USA had joined a peacetime alliance. By 1955 the USSR had set up its own rival organisation – the **Warsaw Pact**.

Key term

Warsaw Pact – a military treaty and association, formed in 1955, of the USSR and its European satellite states

The building of the Berlin Wall, 1961

Revised

By 1959 over 200,000 East Germans were defecting to the West each year through West Berlin. In August 1961 Khrushchev, the leader of the USSR, ordered the construction of a 45-kilometre concrete wall to separate East Berlin from West Berlin. This did solve the Soviets' refugee problem, but at the cost of increasing the tension of the Cold War – President Kennedy promised the people of West Berlin that they would not be taken over by Communism.

Revision task

Use the information in this section to describe America's response to each of these two events:

- The Berlin blockade
- The building of the Berlin Wall

The USA and the Cold War in the wider world

During the 1950s and 1960s the USA became involved in three serious flashpoints of the Cold War – in Korea, Cuba and Vietnam.

The Cuban missile crisis, 1962

Revised

Causes

- In January 1959 the US-backed Cuban dictator Batista was overthrown by a left-wing rebel force led by Fidel Castro.
- Castro ejected all US businesses and investment; the US retaliated by refusing to buy Cuba's biggest export – sugar; the USSR offered to buy the sugar instead.
- Castro now strengthened his relations with the USSR; the threat of a Communist country just 90 miles off the Florida coast worried the new US President John F. Kennedy.
- In April 1961 Kennedy supported a landing of Cuban **exiles** at the Bay of Pigs in Cuba, which was intended to overthrow Castro; it was a disaster and a great humiliation for the US President.
- The Soviet leader, Khrushchev, was concerned about the proximity of US missile bases in Italy and Turkey and wanted to establish Soviet bases in Cuba to balance things out; Castro agreed to his request.

Key events

- On 14 October an American U2 spy plane took photographs of Soviet missile launch sites being constructed on Cuba; Kennedy was faced with several choices:
  - do nothing
  - ask the UN for help
  - invade Cuba
  - attack the Soviet Union
  - blockade Cuba using the US navy.
- Kennedy decided upon the blockade:

20 October	Kennedy imposed a naval blockade around Cuba.
23 October	Khrushchev sent a letter to Kennedy insisting Soviet ships would cross into the blockade zone.
25 October	Kennedy wrote to Khrushchev asking him to withdraw Soviet missiles from Cuba.
26 October	Khrushchev replied saying he would remove the missiles if the US lifted its blockade and agreed not to invade Cuba.
27 October	Khrushchev sent a second letter adding that the US must remove its missiles from Turkey – Kennedy agreed to the first letter in public but the second in private.
28 October	Khrushchev agreed to remove Soviet missiles from Cuba.

Consequences

- Kennedy appeared to have won as Khrushchev had backed down.
- Both Kennedy and Khrushchev were accused of **brinkmanship** – pushing the world to the brink of a nuclear war.
- It was realised that this was too dangerous a game to play and a telephone hotline was installed between the White House and **Kremlin** to ease communication.
- In 1963 a Test Ban Treaty was signed, banning nuclear weapons tests in the atmosphere, under the sea or in space.

Key term

Exile – a person banished from their country of birth

Exam practice

Why was the Cuban missile crisis a turning point in American foreign policy?

[8 marks]

Answers online

Examiner's tip

In this type of question on 'turning points' you need to spell out why a particular event resulted in change. In this instance you need to refer to how the crisis pushed the superpowers to the brink of nuclear war. It was realised that brinkmanship was too dangerous a game to play with nuclear weapons and it resulted in the setting-up of a telephone hot line and the signing of a Test Ban Treaty to control the development of nuclear weapons.

Key terms

Brinkmanship – the policy of pushing a dangerous situation to the brink of disaster

Kremlin – a complex of buildings in central Moscow which forms the headquarters of the government of the USSR

US involvement in Vietnam

Revised

The USA became involved in the war in Vietnam for a number of reasons:

- Vietnam had been a French colony but the French had withdrawn following defeat against Vietnamese forces in 1954.
- Vietnam became divided along the 17th parallel – North Vietnam fell under Communist control under the leadership of Ho Chi Minh, South Vietnam was led by the non-Communist leader Ngo Dinh Diem.
- In 1963 Diem was overthrown and it was feared the Communists would take over the south.
- The US policy of containment meant America had given support to Diem, and the Domino Theory caused America to believe that if South Vietnam became Communist then so would neighbouring Laos and Cambodia.
- The Gulf of Tonkin incident: in August 1964 the US destroyer *Maddox* was fired on by a North Vietnamese patrol boat; President Johnson used this as an excuse to send troops to aid South Vietnam.

US methods of warfare in Vietnam

Revised

- **Operation Rolling Thunder** – an intense bombing campaign of North Vietnam which lasted from 1965 to 1968 with the aim of destroying **Vietcong** supply routes to the south.
- **Chemical warfare** – weapons such as Agent Orange, a chemical defoliant used to destroy the jungle, and napalm, a type of burning jelly, were used.
- **High tech war** – the US used the latest technology: B52 bombers, helicopters, rocket launchers.
- **Increasing troop numbers** – in 1964 there were 180,000 US troops in South Vietnam; by 1968 the number had risen to 540,000.
- **'Search and destroy'** – the US used helicopters to drop troops near villages suspected of assisting the Vietcong; the villages were searched and then set alight which made the US forces unpopular.

Key terms

Vietcong – a Communist guerrilla force that attempted to overthrow the South Vietnam government

Guerrilla war – fighting in small groups against conventional forces, using such methods as sabotage and sudden ambush

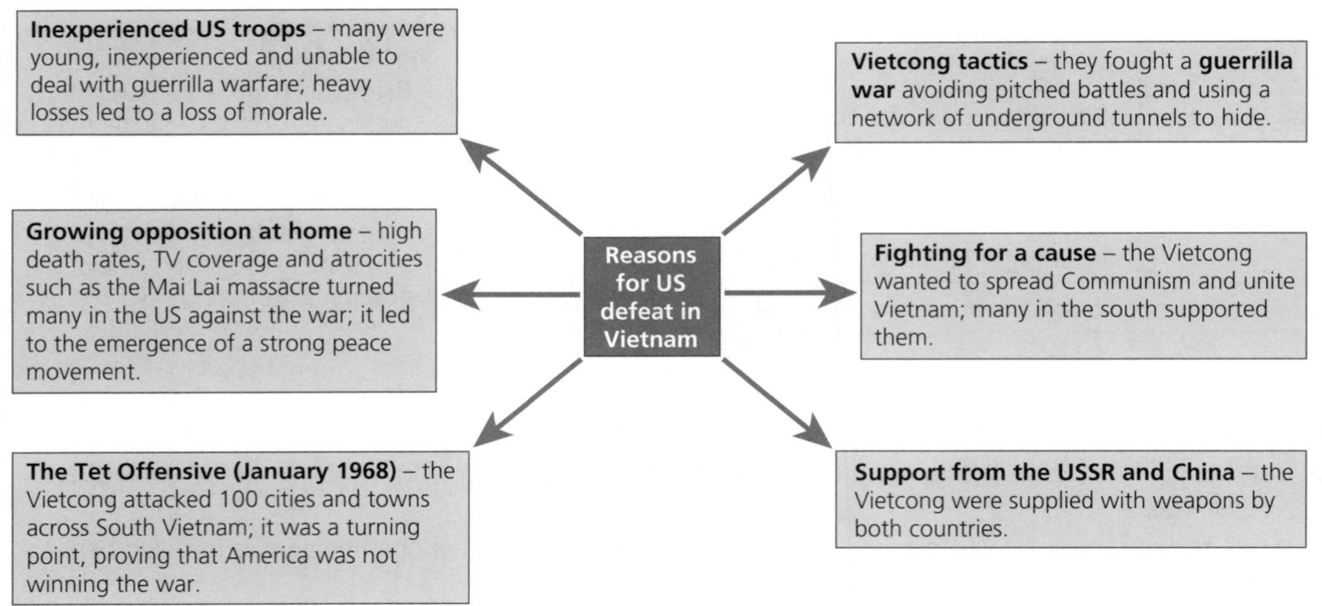

US withdrawal from Vietnam and its consequences

Revised

- Upon entering office in 1969 President Nixon began a policy of **Vietnamisation** and commenced peace talks.
- In 1973 a ceasefire was signed in Paris, followed by a peace treaty, by which time all US troops had left Vietnam.
- North Vietnam was allowed to keep all the land it had captured in South Vietnam.
- By 1975 Communist forces had over-run South Vietnam and in 1976 Vietnam was reunited under the leadership of Ho Chi Minh.
- The US had failed to stop the spread of Communism in South East Asia, and Laos and Cambodia soon turned Communist – the Domino Theory had proved partially true.

Key term

Vietnamisation – US policy of transferring the fighting of the war in Vietnam from American forces to those of South Vietnam

Revision task

Copy and complete the table below. Use the information in this section to evaluate America's performance in the war in Vietnam. In each column, aim to identify **four** factors.

Reasons for US involvement	Methods used by the US forces to fight the war	Reasons for US withdrawal

12.3 What role has the USA played in the search for world peace since 1970?

Improvements in cold war relations during the 1970s

Détente

Revised

The term **détente** is used to describe periods of thaw in cold war relations, primarily between 1971 and 1979. A second period of détente emerged after Mikhail Gorbachev became Soviet leader in 1985.

Key terms

Détente – an attempt to reduce the tension between the USA and USSR

Brezhnev Doctrine – a policy launched in 1968 which called for the use of Warsaw Pact forces to intervene if any Eastern bloc country attempted to rebel against the Communist system

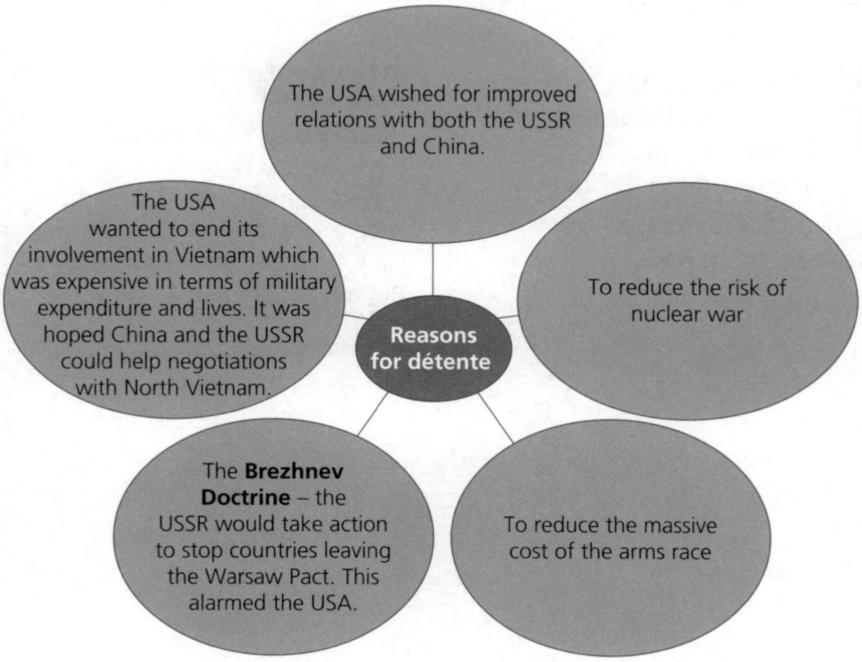

Reasons for détente

- The USA wished for improved relations with both the USSR and China.
- To reduce the risk of nuclear war
- To reduce the massive cost of the arms race
- The **Brezhnev Doctrine** – the USSR would take action to stop countries leaving the Warsaw Pact. This alarmed the USA.
- The USA wanted to end its involvement in Vietnam which was expensive in terms of military expenditure and lives. It was hoped China and the USSR could help negotiations with North Vietnam.

Détente with USSR – SALT I

Revised

- In 1972 President Nixon visited Moscow to improve relations between the USA and USSR.
- Strategic Arms Limitation Talks (SALT) had started in 1969 and this led to the signing of the SALT I agreement in 1972.
- The treaty limited the number of intercontinental missiles (ICBMs) and anti-ballistic missiles (ABMs), and both powers agreed not to test ICBMs and submarine-launched missiles.
- SALT I was important because it was the first agreement between the superpowers to successfully limit the number of nuclear weapons they held.

The Helsinki Agreements, 1975

Revised

In 1975 the USA and USSR, along with 33 other nations, made declarations about international issues:

- **security** – the USA recognised the frontiers of Eastern Europe; the USSR accepted the existence of West Germany
- **human rights** – each signatory agreed to respect basic human rights including the freedoms of thought, speech, religion and unlawful arrest
- **co-operation** – agreements to work towards closer economic, scientific and cultural links.

This new co-operation was shown in 1975 with the docking of the American *Apollo* and Soviet *Soyuz* spacecrafts in space.

Détente with China, 1972

Revised

Several reasons account for improved relations between the USA and China:

- Relations between the USSR and China were strained and Nixon hoped to exploit this split; at the same time China desired more friendly relations with the USA; Nixon also hoped better relations with China would help him to negotiate an end to the war against North Vietnam.
- **'Ping-pong diplomacy'** – the Chinese table-tennis team invited the US team to Peking and the visit in 1971 proved successful and set the scene for improved relations between the countries; in April 1971 the USA lifted its 21-year-old trade embargo with China.
- In February 1972 Nixon became the first US President to visit China – one consequence was improved trading links.
- China was allowed to take its seat at the United Nations in October 1971.

Key term

'Ping-pong diplomacy' – the exchange of table-tennis players between the USA and the People's Republic of China in the early 1970s which helped pave the way for Nixon's visit to China in 1972

The ending of détente – the Soviet invasion of Afghanistan, 1979

Revised

- By June 1979 the USA and USSR were in the final stages of agreeing SALT II which would set further limits on the number of weapons held.
- The US Senate refused to sign up to the SALT II agreement following the Soviet invasion of Afghanistan in December 1979.
- Diplomatic links between the USA and USSR were cut and President Carter stated that the US would use military force if necessary to defend its interests in the Persian Gulf.
- The US Olympic team boycotted the 1980 Moscow Olympic Games; 61 other nations also boycotted them.
- This marked the end of the first period of détente.

Revision task

Show how America's relationship with the USSR and China changed during the 1970s, by describing how the following events changed relations between the superpowers:

- Nixon's visit to Moscow
- SALT I
- Helsinki Agreements
- Ping-pong diplomacy
- Invasion of Afghanistan

US foreign policy during the 1980s and 1990s

Reagan and the second Cold War

Revised

- In January 1981 Reagan replaced Carter as US President and he returned to an aggressive anti-Soviet foreign policy.
- Reagan vastly increased his defence budget and in 1983 US scientists began work on the Strategic Defence Initiative (SDI) or 'Star Wars', developing satellites with lasers that would destroy Soviet missiles in space before they could hit the USA.
- SDI proved a turning point in the Cold War – the USSR, due to its weakening economy, no longer had the money to fund more defence spending to keep up with the USA.

Reagan and Gorbachev – a return to détente

Revised

- In 1985 Gorbachev became the new leader of the USSR and he started a process of reform which included more friendly relations with the USA.
- In November 1985 Reagan and Gorbachev met in Geneva and agreed to speed up arms reduction talks (the Geneva Accord).
- A second meeting was held in Reykjavik in 1986 but negotiations on limitations were slow.
- In December 1987 a third meeting in Washington led to the signing of the Intermediate Nuclear Forces Treaty (INF) by which both leaders agreed to destroy all medium- and short-range weapons in Europe within three years.
- In 1989 the new US President, George Bush Snr, and Gorbachev met at Malta and announced an end to the Cold War.
- At Washington in 1990 Bush Snr and Gorbachev discussed Strategic Arms Limitation (START) and signed the Treaty for the Reduction and Limitation of Strategic Arms (START I) in July 1991.

The ending of the Cold War

Revised

- The reform policies of Gorbachev resulted in the Soviet grip over Eastern Europe loosening.
- In 1989 Gorbachev told the leaders of the six satellite states that Soviet troops would no longer be able to defend them and that members of the Warsaw Pact could make changes to their countries without outside interference.

- Reform quickly spread across the satellite states and the USSR did nothing to stop it.
- Regime change was sparked by the falling of the Berlin Wall in November 1989 and, by the end of 1990, Communist governments had been swept from power in East Germany, Poland, Hungary, Czechoslovakia, Romania and Bulgaria, to be replaced by democratically elected governments.
- These events weakened the USSR and in 1990 the Baltic states of Estonia, Latvia and Lithuania declared themselves independent; in 1991 Gorbachev resigned as leader and the USSR split up into a commonwealth of independent states.
- Europe was no longer divided between Communism and capitalism – the Cold War had ended.

US involvement in Iran, Iraq and the Gulf War

Revised

During the 1980s and 1990s the US became increasingly involved in the Middle East.

Iran

- In January 1979 the Shah of Iran, who had received US backing, was forced to abdicate.
- Iran now fell under the control of a fundamentalist religious leader, the Ayatollah Khomeini, who denounced the USA as the 'Great Satan'.
- In November 1979 the US embassy in Tehran was stormed by Iranian students and 66 Americans were taken hostage; they were held for 444 days.
- President Carter authorised a rescue mission in April 1980 but it failed and it served to worsen relations between the USA and Iran.

The Gulf War (1990–91)

- In August 1990 troops from Iraq invaded and captured neighbouring Kuwait.
- Saddam Hussein, the leader of Iraq, saw Kuwait as a rich prize which would help to lessen his country's economic debts.
- The US wanted to protect its economic interests, especially its oil supplies from this region.
- The United Nations imposed **sanctions** on Iraq. The US, Britain and other states sent forces to protect Saudi Arabia and its oil reserves (Operation Desert Shield).
- In January 1991 the Allies launched an air assault against Iraq (Operation Desert Storm) and in February land forces began the liberation of Kuwait (Operation Desert Saber).
- Saddam was allowed to withdraw with much of his army intact.
- With the defeat of Saddam, President Bush Snr's reputation stood high; America had successfully restored order to the oil-producing states of the Middle East.

Exam practice

How far has America's role in world affairs developed since 1929?

[10 marks + 3 marks for SPaG]

Answers online

Revision task

Draw a timeline to record the key events in American foreign policy between 1980 and 2000. Record events showing improved relationships above the dateline and events showing a deterioration in relationships below the line.

Key term

Sanctions – a penalty usually adopted by several nations acting together against another nation violating international law.

Examiner's tip

In this type of 'synoptic' essay question you need to examine the development of US foreign policy between the years 1929 and 2000, making sure you cover the whole period. In this instance you need to show how America was *inactive* in the 1930s due to isolationism, was forced to become *reactive* in 1941 and then became *proactive* during the Cold War. Since the 1970s America has been active in the search for peace through the policies of détente, the signing of arms reduction treaties and the friendship of Reagan and Gorbachev. Remember not to stop after the Vietnam War – you need to consider events and policies up to 2000!